INVENTORY 1985

INVENTORY 1985

INVENTORY 98

THE WINGS OF THE DOVE

THE WINGS OF THE DOVE
The Story of Gospel Music in America

Lois S. Blackwell

Introduction by Brock Speer

DONNING

Cover design by Fischbach & Edenton, Norfolk, Virginia.

Library of Congress Cataloging in Publication Data:
Blackwell, Lois S.,
The wings of the dove.
Bibliography: p.
Includes index.
1. Gospel music—United States—History and criticism. I. Title.
ML3111.B6   783.7'0973   78-226
ISBN 0-915442-55-8
ISBN 0-915442-50-7 pbk.

Printed in the United States of America

Acknowledgments

For permission to use copyrighted material, I am grateful to the following companies. Any omissions or inaccuracies in the listing are inadvertent, and will be corrected in subsequent editions, provided the publisher is notified.

"Farther Along"—Arr. J. R. Baxter, Jr. Copyright 1937 by Stamps-Baxter Music & Printing Co. in "Starlit Crown." Renewed ©Copyright 1965. All rights reserved. Used by permission.

"Give the World A Smile"—Yandell, arr. Jack Taylor. ©Copyright 1976 by Stamps-Baxter Music of The Zondervan Corporation. All rights reserved. Used by permission.

"He Is Mine and I Am His"—G. T. Speer. Copyright© 1965 by Stamps-Baxter Music & Printing Co. in "Morning Sunbeams." All rights reserved. Used by permission.

"I'll Have A New Life"—Luther G. Presley. Copyright 1940 by Stamps-Baxter Music & Ptg. Co. in "Pearly Gates." Copyright© Renewed 1968. All rights reserved. Used by permission.

"Just A Little Talk With Jesus"—Cleavant Derricks. Copyright© 1937 by The Stamps-Baxter Music Co. in "Harbor Bells No. 6." Renewed ©Copyright 1965 by Stamps-Baxter Music & Printing Co. All rights reserved. Used by permission.

Contents

Introduction

I started singing gospel music with my parents in the summer of 1925. I have continued in gospel music since that time. I have enjoyed many great occasions and had many thrills from this life's work.

Gospel music has changed through the years, especially in the sixties and seventies. Some changes are good and some maybe not so good. The common denominator of the old and the new is the basic four-part vocal sound. This has changed little. The addition of instruments and new electronic devices has enhanced the basic vocal sound in most cases.

In the last few years it has concerned me that the new generation of gospel musicians are not aware of the roots and beginnings of this great music. No definitive work has been written.

Fortunately, some of the old-timers are still living who participated in gospel music in its earlier stages. Lois Blackwell has interviewed many of these veterans and researched the available sources to find out everything possible on the subject. She has attended gospel singings and concerts and gotten the "feel" of the business. She has also examined the ministry of gospel music. She has looked at "old-time" gospel and the "now" gospel.

This book is the result of this research and observation. I am grateful for it.

Gospel music is very dear and very meaningful to me. I feel, when properly performed, it will help cure the ills of the world. I strongly feel that this heritage should be preserved. It is a part of music Americana. This book helps to keep it alive.

Brock Speer, A. B., B. D.
The Speer Family

to the men in my life

Ken, Eric, and Alex

A Note from the Author

A book is written not solely by the author but by the contributions and assistance of many people.

In gratitude I wish to acknowledge all the people in the gospel music industry who have granted me interviews backstage, on fire escapes, at pizza counters, and propped against a Silver Eagle bus.

Brock Speer and Connor Hall gave me much advice and encouragement, and a portion of their time. Tommy Fairchild literally took me by the hand and introduced me to people I might never have otherwise found.

Mr. C. C. Stafford sent me a great deal of helpful material from his own private collection, and directed me to other research sources. Bette Stallnecker provided me with names, addresses, and suggestions which proved invaluable.

I deeply appreciate the time and information given me by the LeFevre family, but even more, I have come to appreciate knowing such wonderful people. Eva Mae and Urias LeFevre have invited me to their home, written letters across the country, and patiently put up with me and my tape recorder for a year. In a letter Eva Mae told me that she thought she had "found a friend." I have found in her, Urias, and Uncle Alph not only dear friends, but beautiful human beings.

Dr. Catherine Marshall graciously invited me into her home and shared with me the memorabilia and materials of Singer's Glen history. My thanks to this warm Southern lady for her help and her hospitality.

I am very grateful to Dr. Robert Trullinger, Director of Humanities at The University of North Carolina—Asheville, for his active assistance in reading, criticizing, and helping to develop this manuscript. His belief in the merit of my work has meant a great deal to me, and I wish most sincerely to thank him.

And, most important of all, I want to thank James Blackwood. If he had not convinced me that I could really do it, I might never have begun this project at all. Through him and his talent I first learned to know gospel music and what it is all about. His influence on me and on the thousands of people that he has touched and affected will make him very special to us forever. I am most grateful for his encouragement and for his revealing to me the true meaning of the gospel song.

Every author comments that it could not have been done "without the cooperation and support of my family." I am not sure that I know an original way in which to express that sentiment, but I do appreciate the nights when Ken, my husband, accepted the quick hamburger casserole when he really wanted fried chicken and milk gravy. And I am grateful for the days when Eric and Alex came to the typewriter to ask if they might go to the basketball game and received, "That's nice, dear," for an answer.

For three years there has been no complaining or griping about the time I have had to spend away from home or about the many hours I have given to library research, letter writing, and the actual composition of this book. Ken hasn't even said anything about the long distance calls on the phone bills.

They have stood around backstage at gospel singings until the early morning hours, and did not fuss about missing dinner or having to accept the only alternative at a greasy spoon.

There were the nights when Ken and the boys were driving me to a sing in a neighboring state and we encountered a complete absence of road signs, a detour that led to the piney backwoods of nowhere, or to a town where no one knew where the high school was located; and an instance when an entire church had been moved and was found only after two hours of questions and wrong answers.

They shared with me the disappointment of traveling several hours only to discover that the singer to be interviewed had become ill and taken a plane home, or that he had not come with his group because of a business appointment.

There have been problems and difficulties, but a lot of it has been fun, too, mostly because they were there. They helped me and they loved me—and I thank them with all my heart.

Lois S. Blackwell

Part I
I'll Meet you in the Morning

On a summer's night in 1972, the city auditorium in Greenville, South Carolina, was crowded with listeners. The Blackwood Brothers Quartet had just performed at an all-night gospel singing. They were the head-lining group with a 40-year reputation in the business. The audience had responded to them enthusiastically, but were yet expectant for what they knew was to come. As the quartet stepped back from the mikes, the piano player broke into the triumphant "King of Kings," and onto the stage strode the man they had all come to see. A progenitor and a pioneer of professional gospel music, he was known to all as a giant of talent and a man of devotion to his field.

James Blackwood walked with just the hint of a strut to center stage. The leonine head was thrown back slightly and the voice was strong and pure. A magnetism was emitted, a spell evolved, and the man sang with a timbre that surrounded the people and made them conscious of him alone. He was short of stature with a fragile and delicate countenance that bordered on the ethereal. But strength was there. The voice projection and the javelin vibrations thrown from his body revealed an inner core of stone that Sisyphus could not have moved.

He sang the songs of his faith and his creed, songs of optimism and hope. At times he would talk to the people, telling them of experiences incurred during the year since he had last been there, speaking of his dreams and plans, his disappointments and sorrows. He spoke of his beliefs and told of his persuasions, and always his testimony encouraged hope and his words were of a joyful expectancy.

He moved down into the audience to sing his personal song of testimony, and his quartet followed, singing also:

> I'll meet you in the morning with a "How do you do,"
> And we'll sit down by the river and with rapture auld acquaintance renew.

His conviction and assurance were infectious, and the people rose to their feet, touched by his obvious joy and his eagerness to share it. From the back, the sides—places beyond his reach—they came forward to shake his hand, wish him

God's blessings, and to unite in this moment of a joyful rapport. Smiles and tears of happiness revealed the satisfaction of being once again assured that a viable God loved and could be loved, and could also give them the comfort and Presence that they might need tomorrow in the canning kitchen or at the doffing machine. An elderly lady, supported by her cane and her own firm conviction, came to embrace the man who made her feel once more the sure and certain hope of a morning beyond her days of arthritic pain and loneliness.

The music continued, the chorus repeated time after time. When Blackwood's voice tired, the quartet would sustain the song until he chose to begin again. Waiting for those who were descending stairs or ramps to reach him, he stepped up on a seat which had been surrendered for that purpose. Costumed in white, he was encircled and transfigured by the spotlight as he raised his hand in greeting and in promise that the joy of which he sang was real. His outstretched hand then touched the people who had been brought to their feet by his music and to his handclasp by the honesty of his warmth and affection.

I'll Meet You in the Morning

I will meet you in the morning by the bright river side,
When all sorrow has drifted away;
I'll be standing at the portals, when the gates open wide,
At the close of life's long, dreary day.

I will meet you in the morning in the sweet by and by,
And exchange the old cross for a crown;
There will be no disappointments and nobody shall die,
In that land e'er the sun go-eth down.

Chorus

I'll meet you in the morning with a "How do you do" and we'll sit down
by the river and with rapture auld acquaintance renew.
You'll know me in the morning, by the smiles that I wear,
When I meet you in the morning, in the city that is built
four square.

James Blackwood's song was over. His promise had been that the faith of their fathers was yet a vibrant and relevant force. The rapport between performer and listener created a sharing, the unique gift that gospel music brings to its followers. Gospel gives its listeners the unusual opportunity to respond and to become very personally involved in its performance. From the carols of the redeemed to the simple tunes of those securely happy, this music has brought to the people a chance to come together, to proclaim their faith and to renew and refresh themselves before returning to handsaws, assembly lines, and dust mops.

The people slowly left, uplifted and ready to face the tomorrows of truculent teenagers, irascible foremen, and—for the youth—a new determination to cope with parents who appeared as aliens in a modern world. A man with the faith and talent to do so, had reaffirmed their beliefs and underlined their hopes.

Without the shared convictions of the people, gospel music would be just another field or type, such as rock or folk or country. The love of the people for the music, for its performers (if they are real and honest), and for the philosophy and almost child-like hope it espouses, is a live and vital force, dormant only until some kindred spirit sings its song. The singing of this song and its listeners' demonstrative response comprise the story of gospel music.

This is a gospel singing. This is what it is all about. Spreading in the past 30 years from a somewhat Southern phenomenon to a national occurrence, gospel has attracted many new devotees and just about as many who don't know what it's all about, and a lot who don't really want to know.

The novice and the uninitiated seem to have two attitudes toward gospel music, complete indifference or total antipathy. The indifferent deem it as a religious fringe to the country field, compatible only with the fundamentalist of the Bible Belt, and consider it probably much like some of the hymn singing they heard in their youth when the Sunday congregation was led by shaky-voiced sopranos and loud off-key deacons from the front pew. To them it is merely an extension of Bible school choruses sung while anticipating the cookies and Kool-Aid, fine perhaps for Sunday morning broadcasting and quite all right for those who are sympathetic and accept its tenets.

Those who hold a definite prejudice against and sometimes even an active animosity toward the music, associate it with the hell-raising tent preachers and extremist sects who use it as a background for their excesses of emotion and absence of decorum or intelligent action in a religious setting. Their hostility is based on experiences of being accosted by street preachers who demand an account of their salvation status and penitent intentions. In their thinking, all adherents of this music carry a pocketful of tracts, awaiting the unwary and probing self-righteous fingers into the recesses of soul, pocketbook, and personal privacy.

In truth, gospel music is a profession born from the church singings of 200 years, welcoming all and besieging none. It is advertised and promoted like any business, but once you buy your gate ticket the expense has ended, for there are no bargain sales for soul saving or hats passed for the singer's mother who is having a cataract operation. If you want to buy a record or song book, that is your business, but there are no special deals in the back room for the naive or the rube.

Gospel is a field of music with its own composers, publishing companies, recording studios, talent agencies, and governing body, the Gospel Music Association. Its entertainers perform at all-night sings, concerts, churches, fairs, in fact just about everywhere except night clubs and casinos. They have pride in their profession and give awards, the Doves, for excellence in the various areas of the field.

Many people dismiss it as simply "religious" music, but on closer inspection its song is born of philosophy as much as religion. One diety is recognized and praised to be sure, but its message goes beyond that. Its precepts accentuate the positive, its canons reveal a hopeful expectancy. Negative thought which infiltrated Judaism and precluded that the Talmud would be a massive volume of "shalt nots," has clouded Christianity despite the Teacher's injunctions toward charity and forgiveness.

Negativism is manifested in the hard shell Baptist's damnations of smoking, drinking, and dancing and in the forbidding edicts issued ex cathedra. Philosophies such as existentialism and nihilism prophesy that all is in vain. Camus' Caligula believed that nothing was important, not even life itself, because all ended in ashes and worms. The world is absurd, nothing can be intrinsically good, and therefore everything is wrong, evil, or unjust. Justice and mercy have no place in the negative thought.

The Puritan fathers punished their people for infractions of inhumane law. Those who could see the hunger beyond the theft and the normalcy of a courting affection rebelled at the restraints of so rigid an order and were repulsed at the cold and merciless branding of a man convicted of a misdemeanor. For them, lightning bolts were not the stigmata of an irate Being renouncing them for their transgressions, but rather a prelude of the rain that trickled down corn stalks and caused the squash vines to green and grow. Believing in love and not judgment, they saw no cause to censure the laughter and frivolous chatter of the young girls as they knelt on river rocks and scrubbed clean the family's wardrobe. The pulpits portended firebrands and demons for the wayward, but if most acts which were normal in a day's living were wayward, then who could escape criticism?

The first brave souls to walk from the Puritan threats to a faith with a promise of love, optimistic hope, and a viable personal experience, founded in this country a religious philosophy based on the tenets that life in and of itself is good and sometimes joyful, that pain and problem can be endured with a sustaining conviction, and that while there is a desire for a new tomorrow, that this world is what we've got to live in, so let's make the best of it.

These philosophizers of over 200 years ago gave birth to American religious folk music and were the ancestors of the gospel singer. The philosophy continues today with no basic changes, and the negativist has once more found the die-hard optimists pounding against the door which he has attempted to board with futility and deleterious action. Cronkite tells us of political scandal, recession, and drought. Ecumenicism harangues dogma, liturgy, and form, and Protestants are again caught in the web of that which we should and that which we should not.

The gospel philosophy offers a simplicity which cannot be confused, and many who are searching again for that which is basic and elemental, find in this clarity an opportunity for an uncomplicated relationship with life, with others, and with themselves. Not a Pollyanna approach of sweetness and light, the message and the method are the same—love God and what He has made, demonstrate in adversity some backbone and grit, and if you feel holy enough to pick up the first stone, then you better step back and think about it for awhile. In short, get in there and live like someone made in a Godlike image and not like an apathetic puppet bumping down the rocky road of life.

Perhaps this line of thought is a simplification of humanism, and perhaps its ordinances and axioms seem superficial and too patent, but the process of stripping away the layers of each culture's dogma until the core of simply being and surviving is exposed as the generating nerve, reduces statutes, not man's stature in the universe. The fundamental gospel philosopher concerns himself only with natural law which he interprets as God's law, and recognizing the existence of forces which he cannot change, he sets his sights on an affirmative course and lives one day at a time, aware of eternity's shadow, but unwilling to cross that bridge until it presents itself. He believes that distant horizon will surpass anything he has ever known anyway, so it portends an ecstasy rather than a fear, and with that anxiety surmounted, he concentrates on improving today and tomorrow as well, as much as it is in his power to do so.

Certainly this philosophy is not for everyone, but it has its disciples and the ranks are growing. Its music evokes the joy of its disciplines, and while it does not propagate itself as an ecstatic balm or a panacea for all ills, it does promise a chance to be happy and an opportunity to share this happiness with others. What is a gospel sing? Friendship, cheer, and hope, and if it is a false hope, then the negativists must have been right after all.

* * *

Americans today aren't given much choice musically. Most radio stations seem to be divided between the acid rock of Led Zeppelin, Aerosmith, and Kiss, or the country sounds of Conway and Loretta and those that sing of "Champagne Lady and Blue Ribbon Baby." Adultery and promiscuity, definitely condoned, are the themes of the steel guitar, while heaven only knows what Ted Nugent and Elton John are saying. Those who listened to the "Hit Parade" fondly remember Nat King Cole, Sinatra, Stafford, and the great show tunes, but about the only way you are going to get to hear "Some Enchanted Evening" nowadays is to own a stereo or tape recorder. The classics are always there and still are very much enjoyed, but sometimes a lighter music is desired and little is being written today that would befit the artistic talents of Crosby, Raitt, Merman, or Mary Martin.

Gospel is one of the very scarce forms of music today in which songs are being composed that are lovely of melody, with lyrics simple yet not contrived, and which tell a story, complete, entire unto itself, and with some significance. One of the main reasons is that the performers in the field are for the most part talented musicians and composers. In the infancy of gospel music, much stress was put on complete musical knowledge. Singing schools were born with the Great Awakening, Normal Schools followed, and in each family where talent was obviously present, lessons were centered around the old upright or pump organ. Brock Speer, son of the founders of the Speer musical dynasty, remembers that from earliest childhood his father, upon discovering some new method or technique in vocalizing or instrumentation, would immediately gather his brood, and all would practice until each could perform the innovation.

Most of the parent generation in gospel music today have backgrounds of formal training, and not just of the shape note variety which all were expected to know, but also in the classical round note theories. In fact, one of the fears of some of these experienced and seasoned performers, is that the young people coming into the business today do not know enough music theory and seem reluctant to learn, satisfied to memorize their parts phonetically. But the leaders in the field are attempting to do something about this, and are working with these kids as did their fathers with them. Teenagers of many of the entertainers are now traveling with the family group during summers and vacation sessions to learn the art by saturation and osmosis.

The performers are artists—knowledgeable, accomplished, and professional—but neither singer, composer, nor publisher defines nor refers to gospel music as an art form. In fact, most gospel people will tell you that what gospel is and what it is meant to be, is not the classical, awe-inspiring music that transcends the ordinary and goes into the ethereal, but rather it is a music spawned from the simplicity of adhering to the basic premise of a life cycle of work, commonplace joys and realistic worries, and an enduring faith. The earmarks of a gospel song are simplicity, optimism, and pragmatic hope. This music was born of and for the people; it continues now in the same tradition, and the day that it forsakes its simple purpose, its death will be tolled by the bells in every church that has sung its song for over 200 years.

Each successful song will have its listeners humming its tune as they leave the auditorium, or harmonizing along as it is aired over the radio. Accentuating the positive in the admonition "that it is ours once to live and once to die," the music stresses the happiness that is possible, acknowledges the hardships and adversities that are unavoidable, but decrees that a person grounded in its dauntless confidence of a well-founded faith, will find if not a roseate, at least a sanguine assurance.

* * *

James Blackwood follows his group aboard the Silver Eagle, going to yet another town, another audience. The pay for his performance was adequate, but certainly insignificant when compared to the fees demanded and received by performers in the rock and country fields. The bus is comfortable, he has his own compartment, but his health is poor. He has followed the black top ribbons for over 40 years. He precipitated the genesis, scouted the early trails, and has firmly established and entrenched his profession. Why does he still stand in the stage wings, eagerly and anxiously awaiting his entrance? His answer to this question is as simple and as basic as his personal philosophy—he loves the music, he loves the people and the opportunity for communion and communication. Talk to any long-time singer of the gospel song, and you will hear reiterated this opinion and dedication to what is truly a labor of love.

The story of this music, the people who were responsible for its deliverance, and of those who carried its song and its tradition to a modern profession, has never completely been told. In the following chapters an attempt has been made to truthfully and factually document the pages of its history, and to tell the story, which is in truth a love story, of the people who sowed the earth by it, who followed casket to grave by it, and who found in its singing, a credence and a sustaining rod for the walkways of everyday life.

Part II
Beginnings and Background

Chapter 1
Emergence of American Folk Hymn

Salt box churches line the rocky coasts of New England, and their inland counterparts jut from the frozen ground in stark memorial to a people long dead. The Puritans had stepped from their boats and had walked from Plymouth to Boston to Cambridge. They built their churches from the slabs of the virgin forests, their villages from their desire for herd-like protection, and from the loneliness of the sea and the pine, so unlike home.

Austere but not grim, they loved their children and they loved God. But after 100 years of plague and disease, Indian threats real and imagined, and the deaths of those most dear, the people realized that their ministers had reached back to the practices of the world from which they had fled. Failing in the original Puritan dream for the New World, of one religion for all and all receptive to that religion, the ministers of Pilgrim descent turned back to clutch the old ways of the Anglican church. Their Calvinistic God did not seem to fit the mold of the raw frontier or the new coastal towns, so they sent for books from England, sent their sons to her universities, and adopted in all ways possible the traits and practices of the English vicar.

Church-going, always a serious business, now was a duty most depressing. The sermons of abstract theology and pointless seminarian arguments were read by the minister, who droned on for two or three hours in an indecipherable monotone. Since there was no heat, the limbs of the worshippers in an hour or so would become numb and cramped, and the hard plank pews were not an advantage of comfort either. An elder would walk among the congregation and sting with his long birch rod any poor soul who had managed to fall asleep despite frozen feet and an aching back.

The law and the correct order of things were the Puritan's guidelines. At times they seemed more interested in their ecclesiastical pecking order of husband over wife, parent over child, minister over member, than in the business of God's world. Rules dictated their every action. On Sundays it was not lawful to play checkers, bake bread, or kiss your wife. Honest and hardworking people, yes—but they had no qualms over slavery or indenture.

Their major requirement for total church membership was conversion through an intense experience to which the individual could testify to the congregation. The flaw in this prerequisite was the absence of opportunity to experience any type of religious emotional feeling. The monotonously read sermons and physical discomforts present in church attendance were not designed to thrill the soul. Puritans preached reason over emotions, so there was never really a time when someone feeling joyful in his faith and confident in his salvation could articulate such emotion, assuming he felt the joy or confidence. As a result, the people did not often feel saved. A concrete experience was a necessity, but it was difficult to find an expression acceptable to ministers and elders, so for the most part the people came to accept the Half-Way Covenant which allowed them attendance in the churches but denied them a communing membership. But in their homes they worried. To each other they vocalized fears stemming from the cold indifference and rigid detachment of their religion, and in the nights they prayed for their souls and for a grace that they didn't know.

Then in 1740 from English shores came George Whitefield. An evangelist and a catalyst, Whitefield had fomented and directed revivals all over England, and with his reputation preceding him, accepted the challenge of American souls. Considered by many to be the first Elmer Gantry in American history, he was viewed by others as a sensitive, persuasive man. The churches, having heard of his successes, opened their doors and pulpits to his message. The message was strict Calvinism and old, but the method was unique to class-conscious ministers and dulled parishioners.

Whitefield preached a personal salvation born from a deep conversion experience, and he preached this doctrine with a fervor and an enthusiasm never before seen. His approach and attitude were very emotional, and his words of a concerned God and an enlivening Spirit caused the people's emotions to soar. Cursing them with hellfire and brimstone if they did not repent, he also promised to the penitent a glorious salvation and a sure and certain hope of eternal life. For the first time the people were caught up in the emotional exhortations of a man of God, and, for the first time, they could personally feel hell's hot breath and the sublime joy of knowing finally that they need not fear its flames: they were saved.

Other ministers followed in Whitefield's wake, and in the next few years revivals were being held in every colony and were attended by large numbers of people of all classes. Some of the hard-back New England clergy were offended by the simplicity and emotional excitement engendered by the evangelists, and they felt that extemporaneous sermons could only lead to a wash of superficial theology. The dubious and the adamant came to be known as the Old Lights, while those advocating the recent reformation were called New Lights. Jonathan Edwards, a Presbyterian minister of Northampton, Massachusetts, was an early disciple and constant preacher of the New Light doctrine. Considered by many to be the greatest theologian America has ever produced, he gave respectability and intelligent thought to the new cause and was the effecter of many converts among the religious New England thinkers.

This evangelistic effort would profit less from the more fanatical preachers who embraced its creed, but not its good sense. James Davenport, an itinerant, would, in the middle of his preaching, strip off his shirt and with huge shouts jump up and down on the platform in an attempt to "stomp out" the devil. Gilbert Tennent chose the disquieting effect of laughing long and hard at the sinners, apparently to intimidate their souls and scare them into salvation.

The antics of such men as these repulsed and offended, to the point of animosity, not only the Old Lights but many of those previously sympathetic to the cause. In succeeding visits to America, Whitefield was frequently met with closed churches and the cold backs of much of the clergy.

But the people could overlook the excesses and be tolerant of the flaws in this reformation, because they felt that God now belonged to them and not just to the ministers with polysyllabic creeds. They traveled as far as was necessary, waited as long as was necessary, and forsook civility in their demand to hear of a God alive and viable. Overflowing meeting houses and homes, they spread into the commons, and heard of their hope for redemption while sitting on the village green. Thus began a practice in this country which was to continue as long as a man loved the land but his God better. Later camp meetings and revivals were set in open fields and flats, ceilinged by the stars and a harvest moon.

This was the Great Awakening. It was a fundamentalist movement, a Renaissance in Calvinism. A revolt against the established order, the Awakening rebelled against the sterile and dehumanizing regime so long enforced by the Puritan leaders. Whitefield and his followers began to publicly question the conviction and sincerity of the ordained clergy. In Whitefield's view, to wear the cloth was not assurance of being permitted to wear the crown. Ministers were required to give testimony of their own conversion, and if the evidence seemed scanty, they were quickly sacked. To sever shepherd from flock was, for many, too extreme, and the movement, splitting and bursting in all directions, carried the seeds and planted the roots of many new denominations. The Old Lights continued on the course of detatched conservatism which led many of their numbers to Unitarianism and Deism.

Increased humanitarianism, particularly toward the Indians and among the abolitionists, and a renewed activity in the mission field were results of the Great Awakening. But one of the most important outcomes of this American reformation was the people's firm grasp on the music of the church, which they now claimed as their own and which they delivered to their children as the heritage of a people in search of their God and His song.

The wooden frame tabernacles of the Puritans had heard only a dreary Psalm-singing, accomplished without organ or harmony. With only about 35 tunes from which to choose, the people had sung uninspired and indifferently, the words of David. A gentleman attending services with his Puritan host was later to comment, "Nor was gloom relieved by gladsome music." This gloom was the gloom of law and punishment unrelieved by love or mercy. If God was a judge and religion a very serious affair, then naturally there was never reason or occasion for a worshipper to smile or experience any joy or happiness in the liturgies of his church.

But the faithful reborn at the revivals were both joyful and hopeful. Salvation was promised them, and they could feel its surge in their hearts. So they turned their backs on the Psalm-singing of their fathers and sought a new music to complement and express their new religion. Taking melodies long familiar in ballads and tavern songs, they added the words of their new-found faith and its hopeful expectations, and the result was the American religious folk song.

John and Charles Wesley, English friends of George Whitefield, wrote lyrics which complemented the open-air preaching of the evangelists.

Songs composed by John Wesley:

Thee Will I Love

Thee will I love, my strength, my tower;
Thee will I love with all my power,
Thee will I love, my joy, my crown;
In all Thy works, and Thee alone;
Thee will I love, till the pure fire
Fill my whole soul with chaste desire.

I thank Thee, uncreated Sun,
That Thy bright beams on me have shined;
I thank Thee, who hast overthrown
My foes, and healed my wounded mind;
I thank Thee, whose enlivening voice
Bids my freed heart in thee rejoice.

Jesus, Thy Blood

Jesus, Thy Blood and righteousness
My beauty are, my glorious dress;
Midst flaming worlds, in these arrayed,
With joy shall I lift up my head.

Bold I stand in that great day,
For who aught to my charge shall lay?
Fully through Thee absolved I am
From sin and fear, from guilt and shame.

Emergence of the American Folk Hymn

Songs by Charles Wesley:

Come, Thou Almighty King

Come, Thou almighty King, Help us Thy name to sing,
Help us to praise! Father all glorious, O'er all victorious,
Come and reign over us, Ancient of Days!

Come Thou incarnate Word, Gird on Thy mighty sword;
Our pray'r attend; Come and Thy people bless,
And give Thy word success;
And let Thy righteousness
To us descend!

Love Divine

Love divine, all loves excelling, Joy of heav'n, to earth come down!
Fix in us Thy humble dwelling, All Thy faithful mercies crown.
Jesus, Thou art all compassion,
Pure unbounded love Thou art;
Visit us with Thy salvation, Enter ev'ry trembling heart.

Come, almighty to deliver, Let us all Thy life receive;
Suddenly return, and never, Never more Thy temples leave.
Thee we would be always blessing,
Serve Thee as Thy hosts above,
Pray, and praise Thee without ceasing, Glory in Thy precious love.

Isaac Watts articulated for the people the music and faith they now felt.

When I Survey the Wondrous Cross

When I survey the wondrous cross
On which the Prince of Glory died,
My richest gain I count but loss
And pour contempt on all my pride.

Forbid it, Lord, that I should boast
Save in the death of Christ, my God;
All the vain things that charm me most,
I sacrifice them to His blood.

O God, Our Help in Ages Past

O God, our help in ages past,
Our hope for years to come,
Our shelter from the stormy blast,
And our eternal home:

Under the shadow of Thy throne
Thy saints have dwelt secure;
Sufficient is Thine arm alone,
And our defence is sure.

Composers such as William Cowper penned the words and the people sang of things now very real to them. They sang of Satan and salvation, of baptism and a tempting life, of eternity and hope.

There is a Fountain

There is a fountain filled with blood
Drawn from Immanuel's veins;
And sinners, plunged beneath that flood,
Lose all their guilty stains.

The dying thief rejoiced to see
That fountain in his day;
And there have I, as vile as he,
Washed all my sins away.

God Moves in a Mysterious Way

God moves in a mysterious way
His wonders to perform;
He plants His footsteps in the sea,
And rides upon the storm.

Judge not the Lord by feeble sense,
But trust Him for His grace;
Behind a frowning Providence
He hides a smiling face.

Songs were entitled for a geographical location of special significance to the writer, or to honor someone respected and loved. "Pisgah," "Concord," "Olney," "Vernon," "Dunlap's Creek," "Leander," and "Lennox" were songs cherished and passed from generation to generation.

As far as is known, the first American religious folk song was "Wicked Polly," reputedly sung at the funeral of a wayward girl in Little Rest, Rhode Island, and fitted to different tunes down through the years. *The Folk Songs of*

North America by Alan Lomax comments: "Her [Polly's] story, set to an old ballad air, caught the imagination of folk. It was reprinted in a score of rural song-books...and it is still sung by Southern Hard Shell Baptists as a warning to their gallivanting daughters." Here is the first line of this song of warning:

> Young people who delight in sin,
> I'll tell you what has lately been:
> A woman who was young and fair
> Died in sin and deep despair.

"Romish Lady" is another of the oldest, describing the fortune of a Roman Catholic girl who turns from the papacy to Protestantism and creates her doom at the stake. The martyr's story is sung in eleven long verses, but a taste of the faith and perils of the "Romish Lady" can be found in these stanzas:

> There was a Romish lady, Brought up in popery,
> Her mother always taught her, The priest she must obey
> "O pardon me, dear mother, I humbly pray thee now,
> But unto these false idols I can no longer bow."
>
> . . . .
>
> "O take from me these idols, remove them from my sight;
> Restore to me my Bible, wherin I take delight!
> Alas, my aged mother, why on my ruin bent?
> 'Twas you that did betray me, but I am innocent.
>
> "Tormentors, use your pleasure, and do as you think best;
> I hope my blessed Jesus will take my soul to rest."
> Soon as these words were spoken, up steps the men of death,
> And kindled up the fire to stop her mortal breath.

Two things happened which were to greatly effect and influence this folk music. In 1798 Smith and Little published a songbook entitled, *The Easy Instructor.* It was unique for two reasons. The music was written out in notes and these were shaped rather than round. "Round" notes are simply those notes which all composers have used for centuries in the writing of their music. The standard ABCDEFG of the keyboard of a piano is, of course, utilized by all musical instruments, and has been through the ages. However, the shape note system is unique in that upon seeing a note on a songsheet, one doesn't have to be able to read music in the classic sense, but can recognize the sound that each shape note represents merely by its form. For this reason, singers who are familiar with shape notes can look at the notations and know that the melody is structured by the sounds the shape notes represent. Rather than singing "ah" or the distinction of a "B," the shape notes directly transmit fa, sol, la, and mi. Having few or no hymnals, the Puritans had had to satisfy themselves by singing while the minister or an elder "lined-out" the words of the song. Finally, in 1721, *Grounds and Rules of Musick* appeared, the first book in the colonies to use regular notes to provide the accompanying melody along with the lyrics. But this was largely a volume of instruction and technique, which contained only the Psalm hymns of which the people had grown weary.

The Easy Instructor took the old fasola system, used as long ago as the days of Shakespeare, and attaching a different shape note for each sound, printed a song in a technique so simple that it could be quickly learned by any singer. According to *White Spirituals in the Southern Uplands* by George Pullen Jackson: "So the series with which we are more or less familiar nowadays . . . was sung fa sol la fa sol la mi fa in Shakespeare's England, and is still so taught and practiced among those who belong to this lost tonal tribe in America."

As can be seen, this method uses only four of the seven sounds heard universally today. Do re mi fa sol la si do was condensed to the four fa sol la mi shape note system reminiscent of the Shakespearean style. The melodies were limited with only the four sounds, but this was no loss to a people who had never before had any selection in their music. *The Easy Instructor* contained instructions and method, but it also included songs that now could be sung more readily with the new system.

Soon after the seeds of religious division had scattered, the new denominations and a few of the old, Baptist, Methodist, Shaker, and the Church of God, joined in a common trait, the love of the livelier and more relevant church music. Songs now spoke of the hardships of a life of labor in the field or the shop, of the particular pain of those who fail and fail but try once again, of the strength and endurance of those bent but unbowed. Ignorant of musical knowledge, but emboldened by their desire to sing a joyful song, each congregation of the New Lights sang of a hard life and a merciful God to tunes that had once been fiddle breakdowns and dance accompaniments to reels and waltzes.

The second occurrence which was to have a profound effect on the folk music was the advent of the singing schools, believed by some to have started as early as 1770. The singing teacher, much like the circuit preacher of a later day, guided his hammerhead mule from path to road and led the people from congregation to choir. Sometimes he would stop at a local inn, or preferably stay with a family from the church. For two weeks or maybe three, he would instruct each night, teaching the notes, harmony, and meter. The students learned to sing the syllables represented by the notes before attempting to combine lyrics and melody. This is a practice still used today in *Sacred Harp, Christian Harmony,* and gospel singings in the South.

The people began to sing in parts. With the simplified four note system and the new song books being published, they could learn a fairly complicated harmony easily. In 1805 Jeramiah Ingall published his *Christian Harmony,* not to be confused with Billy Walker's later book of the same name, and in 1815 Aninias Davisson brought out the *Kentucky Harmony.* While before all hymns were sung in unison, with the masculine bass adding the only diversion, now there was a distinct four-part harmony. Tenor was sung by the high-voiced men and/or women, the counter or soprano could be sung by either sex and contained quite often, although not always, the melody. The treble or alto was left to the women, and, of course, the men sang bass.

Other song books appeared, all using Little and Smith's fasola shape note system. The *Missouri Harmony* was used by Abraham Lincoln in later years, and for nearly two centuries people have used the *Columbian Harp*, the *Sacred Harp*, and the *Southern Harmony*. These books were shaped differently from our songbooks today. They were oblong, usually in size about eight by five inches. Each contained a front section composed of the explanation of terms and the rudiments of music. The songs were divided usually into three parts: hymns for church use, slightly more informal ones for Sunday School and revivals, and in the back, anthems for the choir.

The pastoral and picturesque setting of the Shenandoah Valley became the background for a printing company which was to wax influential in the heritage of religious music. Joseph Funk, grandson of the first Mennonite bishop in the United States, moved to the valley with his family at the age of ten. Little is known of his early life, but it is certain that he was an intelligent and knowledgeable man. Versed in Latin, as well as his family tongue—German— Funk published in 1816 a songbook, *Choral-Music*, written in German. Sixteen years later his *Genuine Church Music* was printed in English, signifying the Anglicization of his neighbors and indicative of an early interest of many Mennonites in this form of religious music.

However, Joseph Funk was soon to become alienated from the Mennonite faith due to his love for and interest in musical instruments. The plain people did not permit any type of instrument in their church, not even piano or organ. Funk and his children joined the Baptist church, as did their descendants after them, and here began the generations of a musical people who shared their love through the books they published. The tiny village in which Funk's family had settled had been called Mountain Valley, but when progress caused a post office to be built there, it was discovered that another Virginia town had already laid claim to that name, so with Mr. Funk's influence, this bit of mountain greenery came to be called Singer's Glen.

Joseph Funk's great, great granddaughter, Dr. Catherine Marshall, lives today in Singer's Glen. A historian in her own right, Dr. Marshall carefully preserves the records and heritage of her family, and possesses a photograph of the famous Funk seated at an organ with the other members of the Singer's Glen orchestra surrounding him—a well-known local physician with violin in hand, more fiddles, guitars, and various instruments, for the love of which Funk forsook the German ways and established a Baptist dynasty so total that one later descendant, a great-niece, is remembered in the family because the lady was a Lutheran and "was different because she was sprinkled, you know."

Many songs were composed as well as published in this Virginia valley, but Singer's Glen came to the height of its fame after the Civil War with Funk's grandson, Aldine Kieffer. His story is related a little later.

One of the earliest types of songs to become immensely popular was the fugue. The fuguing songs were written for the most part by William Billings, a New Englander who lived from 1746 to 1800. Billings' "When Jesus Wept," a canon of four parts, appeared in 1770 in *The New England Psalm-Singer*, according to *The American Heritage Songbook*, edited by Leish and Folds. His songs are to be found in most of the fasola books and are still sung by the *Sacred*

Harp and *Christian Harmony* enthusiasts. The fugue was comprised of one set of lyrics and a four-part harmony, each voice part commencing slightly after the one preceding. Jacob Kimball in his *Rural Harmony* newspaper in 1793 made this observation: "In fuguing music, the strength of the voices should increase as the parts fall in." This produced an effect most striking. Perhaps it would appear merely noisy or cacophonous to the unaccustomed ear, but a congregation of strong voice and fuguing talent presents an impressive musical experience. Billings' songs remained quite popular in most circles until after the Civil War, when only the steadfast few of the fasola disciples continued in the fuguing tradition.

All of the songbook publishers mentioned were also singing teachers who packed their Bibles and clean socks in their saddle bags and rode through the elements to take their songs to the people. Chicken and dumplings and country ham dinners awaited the teachers after class. These itinerant musicians were anticipated most eagerly and were welcome visitors. Not just the papas and mamas, but also the children attended the lessons, and went home to practice what they had learned. From these singing schools sprang the roots of a way of life and a type of singing that live today wherever gospel is sung.

Some of the songs were sad, dealing with parting and death, others were more optimistic. But while some dealt with death, it was never in the pessimistic light that the Negroes saw and reflected in their spirituals. To the white singer, while the separation of death might be sorrowful, there was always a hope of another and better life. The Negro, fettered and hopeless, saw in death only another fearsome unknown, and therefore sang as if there were no promise of tomorrow. Alan Lomax's *The Folk Songs of North America*, states "White hymns normally look on death as a joyous release from sin and sorrow; only in Negro spirituals does death appear as an uncertain blessing or an enemy." Heaven, for the blacks, was a dream, not a reality of which they could be sure.

Many people, in error, have believed that gospel music was a direct descendant of the Negro spirituals. This is totally untrue. The Negroes sang melodies of sorrow born of their own invention and often with Afro-traces of the past. In some instances, they borrowed the master's tunes and improvised their own lyrics. While some of the spirituals reflect their moments of happiness, many of them fall into the category of which Oscar Hammerstein II was later to write— the "I'm tired of living, but scared of dying" pessimism. The slave owners held death as the final punishment, and the preachers claimed God for the whites, so an inevitable uncertainty concerning the afterlife caused the Negroes to despair of and to question any hope of a blissful eternity.

Another comment from Lomax is, "Negro and white spirituals share similar Biblical symbolism, it is true, but, in examining the now extensive collections of white spirituals we have yet to find *any* songs with the explicit sorrow over the actual woes of this world, with the explicit anger against oppression, and with the ringing cries for freedom to be discovered in the Negro songs."

As has been seen, the religious folk songs sung by the whites were born in their revivals and reformations, and evolved into the gospel songs which were being published by 1877. Their direct lineage sprang from music composed to comply with the religious feeling of the day, and then was wedded to melodies of long use.

The tune of the folk hymn "Mount Watson" is almost identical to the old ballads "The Poor Little Fisherman Girl" and "Green Willow." "Wondrous Love," one of the most loved and enduring hymns, got its melody from the unlikely "Captain Kidd," a salty tavern song. "When Boys Go A-Courting" became "John Adkins' Farewell," a folk song entreating its listeners to turn from the evils of drink to more Christian attributes. "Sailor's Home," whose lines proclaim divine protection from the dangers of the deep, got its tune from the old classic "Lord Lovel," which itself is similiar to another classic, "Barbara Allen."

Negro gospel music exists today as an entirely separate and different field from white gospel, although in the past year inroads have been made in combining the two styles in various forms of entertainment. However, black roots burrow back into the days of bondage and oppression, and it would be difficult to imagine that white listeners or singers could ever completely empathize with the feelings that the black music conveys. The two forms of gospel music grew side by side in this country—separate entities, kindred only in a basic fundamental foundation, the shared faith in a living God.

The singing schools began in New England and New York and grew eastward to Pennsylvania, west to Cleveland, Cincinnati, and St. Louis, and south through the Shenandoah Valley. Billy Walker of Spartanburg, South Carolina, in 1935 published the South's first book of religious folk songs, *The Southern Harmony.* In the four shape note system, this book held many of the old songs which had never before been committed to paper. Songs remembered by grandmothers and taught in the oral tradition were now printed for all to learn and sing. Old familiar tunes such as "Turkey in the Straw," "Barbara Allen," and "O Susannah" had been in years past fitted with religious words and had served sometimes several different texts before the people finally determined on one particular set of lyrics for one melody.

Walker, also a teacher and composer, claimed to have sold 600,000 books before 1854, and he was probably telling the truth; the people loved the old songs, and the fasola music made the parts melodically more interesting. It was also a little faster; there were more notes to the minute. While there were a few slight differences between the singing of the North and the South, singers in both areas could add a little musical ornamentation to the songs, and the songbook pages showed only a fraction of what they sang. This ability to emboss a song as they sang it, plus their remarkable talent for sight reading, was to confound their researchers in later years. They could then, and they can today, pick up a new book, never before seen by them, and begin singing in perfect four-part harmony, adding and embellishing as they go along. This is an innate talent, born from a visceral passion and nurtured from a shape note *en rapport.*

The conventions saw their genesis along with the singing schools. At the completion of each school, the pupils would have a concert to demonstrate to relatives and neighbors their advanced musical abilities. These student singings were so much fun for performer and listener alike, that each church began having convention sings at regular periods. Soon singers from one church were invited to sing at a neighboring congregation, and eventually the conventions were held every month or so at a designated site with the whole county in attendance.

And, of course, the most favored time for the popular and well-attended sings was Sunday afternoon. In the days before movies, television, and radio, and with many blue laws in effect, plus the fundamentalist censure against work or irreverent play, the Sunday singing provided about the only opportunity for entertainment. There was an added inducement for the older folk, a chance to socialize and catch up on conversation, and for the younger ones— a day with their beaus and a sanctioned arena for sparking.

The mid-day feasts assembled by the ladies were not to be despised either: Kansas Maid cloth, gaily colored and smelling of soap and sunshine, covered baskets of fried chicken, butter beans, and biscuits. Their culinary talents at stake, the women produced sugar-glazed ham which competed with pans of rich sage dressing smothered with juicy slices of white turkey. Cakes were given a corner-of-the-eye inspection for height and thickness of jam toppings and coconut-stacked peaks. The wooden barrel gave a fountain of ice cold lemonade, and the butter-drenched vegetables and crusty pies created the temptation to eat too much and too well. Food was a basic and necessary pursuit of much of their daily labor, and so it naturally became a source of much of their pleasure.

Their God, their music, their way of life and its harvests, comprised their universe, and for them this was enough; it was good.

Chapter 2
The Camp Meeting Song

The people loved their music and it was a love that they shared. The first camp meeting in Logan County, Kentucky, in 1800 began a sharing experience that has continued to this day. Camp meetings drew the saints and the sinners, the believers and the backsliders, into a commune of hell-fire preaching, knee-slapping singing, and hand-shaking sociability.

Toward the open flats or fields, people came from as much as two or three days distance from their homes. Traveling the miles in covered wagons and buckboards, the families with babies and young children were conspicuous by the fresh cow tied to the tailgate. For a meeting of two weeks or longer, farmers often latched coops of frying chickens, and if they were so fortunate, cured hams and shoulders to their wagons. It was always obvious where the best meals would be served. Mules or oxen pulled the family cargo, which included feather bedding covered with ticking, wool blankets to ward off the cold of the forest night, such clothing as the family had, and all the finery they owned, which might consist of an aged silk dress, a piece of lace, or a tortoise shell comb.

Sites were chosen for their proximity to water, and camps were set up on the banks of a river or creek. Wood smoke soon filled the air, and with it was mingled the smell of side meat frying and coffee boiling. Bread dough was wrapped on sticks or placed on flat rocks to bake, and with a couple of potatoes fried in the meat grease, supper was soon prepared.

Visiting from wagon to tent was one of the main inducements of a camp meeting. Courtships were begun as the evening cooled the ground and the mists began to rise. Sometimes a shrill scream would pierce through the wood smoke and fog, and a new singer would be born, named for a minister or perhaps a river, and so honored since he had had the good sense to be delivered at so propitious a time.

A large platform was built in the middle of the open ground, high enough so that all could see. There were always at least two or three preachers to conduct the meeting, and in this way, with one parson concentrating on south and south-west, and another the north, and yet another the east, each section of the crowd had a personal speaker and song leader. This was mandatory for the large numbers that attended each meeting.

At night, pine knot torches were placed around the platform, affording light and an unwanted amount of heat. As the evangelists more vigorously admonished the unrepentant, sweat rolled down their faces and into their eyes. Coats and collars were shed; cambray shirts were unbuttoned and held in place by leather galluses. Excitement spread through the people as their sins were defined and their salvation promised. If one preacher was caught up in the passion of his own oratory and trespassed on a brother's territory, no one seemed to notice or to mind very much. Often a section of the crowd might be receiving the benefits of two or all three of the ministers.

There was some excess of emotion at a meeting from time to time. The Holy Rollers would put on an exhibition of shakes, rolls, and mouth frothing occasionally, but for the most part, camp meetings were attended by basic fundamentalists who thought a show of either contrition or elation should be confined to rousing "hallelujahs" and sincere "praise the Lords." These people were Baptists, Methodists, and Presbyterians for the most part, with a few participants from other sects. And certainly if there were to be two Presbyterian preachers at a meeting, you could count on a big turn-out of Scots-sired attenders. But the Methodists and Baptists came as well to hear what the disciples of Knox had to say.

Upon the spirals of white ash smoke, touching the pinnacle tips of sycamore and oak, came a burst of song as free and unfettered as were the hearts of the people who sang it. The camp meeting song was born in the sweat and fear of the late hour prophesier, and in the love and relief of the pardoned and redeemed. Anxiety and insecurity were ended, the step was taken, the covenant was made.

Accepting the grace and mercy, they pledged their loyalty and their lives. The song became joyous; it burst through the night and soared on free wings. The people stood with faces in the wind and sang praises to their God.

The flames of the torch fires danced, and the people huddled together as the cold winds swept through the forests and out onto the flat. Screech owls and raccoons babbled over the invasion of their domain; the wolves feared the great numbers and their fires, and circled back to the mountains. Woolen shawls and knitted scarves were drawn closer over throats now swollen with song. Children, long asleep on their mothers' shirts, heard the wind and, although afraid, rolled their eyes to see the clouds sweep across the sky in its wake. Wisps of gray hair blew loose from the grandma's knot and flogged her face as she strained to see through the stars to heaven's portals. They sang of death defied and the morning assured. The wind caught these songs, but found that it had no firm hold, and the songs went back to the people.

The fervor and excitement of the camp meetings are visible in those songs which were produced by torch light and contagious zeal.

> There's glory, glory in my soul,
> It came from heav'n above;
> Which makes me praise my God so bold,
> And His dear children love.
>
> O give Him glory, O give Him glory,
> O give Him glory, for glory is His own,
> And I will give Him glory, and I will give Him glory,
> Arise and give Him glory, for glory is His own.

In *White Spirituals in the Southern Uplands* by George Pullen Jackson, the analogy of the people's pilgrimage to the camp ground and to their final journey is made. "The camp-meeting hymn is not churchly, but the companionships of the rough journey to the camp reappear in songs of a common pilgrimage to Canaan, the meeting and partings on the ground typify the reunion of believers in heaven...." This analogy is seen in the following camp song:

> I'm glad I ever saw the day
> We met to sing and preach and pray.
> Here's glory, glory in my soul
> Which makes me praise my Lord so bold.
>
> Lord keep us safe while pressing through,
> And fill our souls with meekness too.
> Redeeming grace, that pleasing song,
> We'll sing as we do pass along.
>
> I hope to praise Him when I die
> And shout salvation as I fly.
> Sing glory, glory through the air,
> Meet all my Father's children there.

—Found in *Melody of the Heart*, 1804, Abner Jones, publisher

Repetition is seen in several of the lines of the two songs. Working with such large numbers, the song leaders had to keep the lyrics simple and often repeat so that all could sing. Repetition songs themselves were very popular, such as this song:

> O brothers will you meet me,
> On Canaan's happy shore?

> —*Hymns and Spiritual Songs,* 1806, Mintz, publisher

The response to this was:

> By the grace of God I'll meet you (*sung three times*)
> Where parting is no more.

Many verses were involved in this type of song, going on to include sisters, mothers, fathers, mourners, and as many categories as the song leader could improvise.

But the main emphasis in all camp meeting songs was on personal salvation. Quoting again from Lomax: "The common man, the individual, is everything in American folk song. The folk spirituals—in contrast to older types of hymns—sing mainly of personal salvation."

One camp song that has become in part a favorite Easter hymn for many churches is the joyous:

Shout On or *Antioch*

> I know that my redeemer lives,
>> Glory Hallelujah!
> What comfort this sweet sentence gives!
>> Glory Hallelujah!

> Shout on, pray on, we're gaining ground,
>> Glory Hallelujah!
> The dead's alive and the lost is found,
>> Glory Hallelujah!

> —*Daniel Medley,* 1784

The fires of the Great Awakening had, after a few short years, flickered and seemed nearly extinguished. But the advent of the camp meetings revitalized the religious zeal among the Protestants, especially in what were then the West and the South. In New England the New Lights were never completely extinguished. Some of the dissenters once more recanted and were blended back into the formalized and structured churches, but their Calvanistic brand is in evidence even today in the liturgical churches of New England. This brand, which once burned through their sterile dogma, lingers, and its charred remains ignite and come to life if touched by the melody of a song once free.

But in the West and South the revival fires caught and spread to the frontier's edges. Ontario County in New York state was referred to in later years as the "burned over area," due to the repeated evangelist meetings held in the first few years of the nineteenth century. People questioned their denominations, their ministers, and each other. Seeking the truth, they would travel great distances in discomfort and danger to hear a new preacher, one who was said to hold the secrets of God's will. Thus they came to the camp meetings—for fellowship, yes, and for recreation—but primarily they came in search of a God who, when He did speak, could make them hear.

The genesis of the camp meeting song opened a new chapter in the story of gospel music. Literally taking the old songs and singing them to pieces, the people inadvertently created the gospel chorus. Taking a couple of familiar lines and adding appropriate exclaimers such as "hallelujah," the minister could lead his proportioned section in singing. Even with the loose divisions, the crowd would be so large that it was impossible to try to teach them a new song, and with a free mating of a set of lyrics to any tune desired, there wasn't a majority to agree on any one particular melody.

Some leaders attempted the old Puritan method of "lining out" a song for their groups, but it was difficult to be heard above the din of the dog bark and the infant cry, and anyway you just can't sing a song you don't know with the same abandon and enthusiasm that you do if the song is a dear old friend. There were no books except the few that belonged to the people who came, so on-the-spot inprovisations created new songs that held the spicy flavor prevalent only in a camp meeting song.

As time went on, the shape note singing schools began to have a tremendous effect on the meetings. The graduates of these classes, who assembled at meeting time, knew the repertoire of their teachers, and had in common many new songs to share. These were salted with camp meeting savor, and the people sang them with great gusto and feeling.

Refrains and choruses were often disjointed and seemingly not related, due to the larger masses singing the most familiar chorus and a few joining in on the verses. The choruses were then embellished and often elongated until they were themselves a whole song. Wild and free were the songs of praise. The last verse of "Shout Glory" follows:

> Yes, praise the Lord, we'll rise and tell
> The wonders of Immanuel;
> He sav'd our souls from death and hell—
> We love to tell the story.

"Tis the Very Same Jesus" is a good example of a simple chorus which became an entire song:

> Tis the very same Jesus,
> Tis the very same Jesus,
> Tis the very same Jesus, the Jews crucified.
> But He rose, He rose,
> He rose and went to heaven in a cloud.

The joy and the promise given the people are obvious in "Glorious Morning":

> Glorious morning, happy morning of the Lord,
> And we'll all rise together in that morning.
> The preacher will be there, and his people will be there,
> And they'll all rise together in that morning.

The song goes on with leaders and members, the Father and His children, etc., for as many verses as the singers have sufficient stamina and imagination.

The answer to the old song "And Am I Born to Die?" is "Better Day Coming":

> I'm glad that I am born to die,
> From Grief and woe my soul shall fly;
> For there's a better day (a)coming,
> Will you go along with me?
> For there's a better day (a)coming,
> I'll go sound the jubilee.

And from Billy Walker's *Southern Harmony* comes a camp meeting song loved and sung for many years before Walker finally committed it to paper:

Midnight Cry
(last verse)

> When earth and sea shall be no more,
> And all their glory perish,
> When sun and moon shall cease to shine,
> And stars at midnight languish;
> When Gabriel's trump shall sound aloud,
> To call the slumbering nations,
> Then, Christians, we shall see our God,
> The God of our salvation.

The camp meeting was carried by its disciples into the twentieth century, and the camp and brush arbor meetings continued in the rural South until technology and industrialization replaced the live experience with the 21-inch program and the cartridge tape.

Chapter 3
Singer's Glen

The frontiers spread to the Mississippi and beyond. Immigrants stepped on American soil in New York, Boston, and Newport, and swelled the wagon trains bound for California and the Santa Fe Trail, for Sutter's Mill and Donner's Pass. Others stayed behind to work in the sweat shops and mills provided by the Industrial Revolution. Albany, Chicago, and Cleveland grew from towns to large urban centers of trade and business; the South whispered war behind swansdown fans, and the North looked to entrepreneurs and abolitionists for support. Indian tribes were ravaged and displaced, and the humanitarianism born during the Great Awakening disappeared. Johnny Rebs, Yankee boys, and red men were all shot with a vengeance. And if a man's hands were bloody, his rationalization was as close as the underground railroad or the settler's massacre.

As the country grew and the cities grew, the proud new owners of an urban home were suddenly ashamed of their rural religion and its salty earth music. The days of bustles and beaver hats were becoming increasingly more sophisticated, and believing that education, culture, and anything worthwhile came from Europe, the clerks and factory workers feigned the detached attitude of the wealthy Anglican or Roman Catholic. By the time the land showed its first scars from the Civil War, the city churches had forsaken the folk music of their heritage and had reverted to the more formal services with the dusty tunes of the monks and crusaders. Only in the South did the singers still convene to sing the old and to write the new songs that grew from their tenacity and faith.

The division between the urban and the rural churches' choice of music is reflected in this passage from *Music in America*, by John Rublowsky: "On one side were the traditionalists who looked to the Old World and lamented the changes that occurred in the 'old sacred melodies.' On the other, was the great mass of people who, untutored and unlettered, made music for the sheer joy of the experience. This music reflected and expressed their lives. It developed a distinctive cadence and style that was different from that of the past. The traditionalists sneered at their innovations and dubbed their style with the name 'common.' "

The economy was booming as it can only just before or during a war. The brownstone residents and the tenement dwellers could both afford their idea of the current European fashions, and where better to show them off than the Sunday stroll to church and the long walk home through the park and down the avenues. Congregations were no longer made up primarily of salvation seekers; there were now more varied reasons for church attendance. It was good for business and became an arena for buyers and sellers. Episcopalians were affluent, or soon hoped to be. In *The National Experience: Part I:* "After the Revolution the Protestant Episcopal Church...grew slowly, appealing mostly to well-to-do Eastern conservatives."

The Congregationalists and Presbyterians were just a cut under, and achieved more success in their proselytizing, while the immigrant Lutherans were considered definitely "middle-class" and not to be involved in the financial scheme of things. Although comprising the larger congregations, the Baptists and Methodists were either rural dwellers, or the urban bottom of the social church ladder. The various new splinter sects again were for the most part farmers, and not class contenders.

Paul Henry Lang's *One Hundred Years of Music in America* makes this observation: "Already by mid-century [nineteenth] the denominations had so drawn their social lines that some ministered to the wealthy and elite in big cities, while others served the common folk on farms and frontiers."

Europe influenced us with her music, and Handel and Mozart were acceptable, while Watts, Newton, and Wesley were not. The large urban churches, to be assured of an adequate liturgist and harmonious choir, had begun to hire singers and musicians, a practice abhorred by their country counterparts.

About this time, three hymn writers began to compose and publish a middle-of-the-road religious music. Lowell Mason (1792-1872), Thomas Hastings (1784-1872), and William Bradbury standardized the Protestant hymn into the form in which it is now universally accepted. Mason introduced singing classes in the public schools and also in the liberal arts colleges in the mid-West for the purpose of training teachers. He was the author of "Nearer My God to Thee." Hastings gave us "Rock of Ages" and "Guide Me O Thou Great Jehovah," while Bradbury composed these enduring favorites: "Just As I Am," "Sweet Hour of Prayer," "He Leadeth Me," and "Savior Like a Shepherd Lead Us."

These men were influential and respected in their field, but unfortunately, they were very much opposed to the old folk hymn and the camp meeting song. They felt that each was a nasal music with "uncertainty" of pitch, and they deplored the fact that they were often sung without organ or any instrumental accompaniment. They were equally offended by the shape note system and believed it an inferior form of music. Today, sophisticated church musicians regard the hymns of these men as being without true merit and worth musically, and would prefer to see them weeded from the hymnals of their churches.

But the European influence, in one way, had a very positive effect on America's religious music. This influence encouraged the use of the do-re-mi system rather than the old fasola, and many writers attempted to devise a seven shape note system which was practical and applicable. In 1846 *The Christian Minstrel* by Jesse B. Aiken was published in Philadelphia. In this book Aiken presented his version of the seven-note plan which is used universally today.

This was an important step in the growth of gospel music, perhaps the most important. For now it was possible for all the singers of the old folk music to have a common note system, yet one that afforded them the most range and maneuverability musically. The acceptance of this system by the rural churches deepened the gulf between them and the larger urban congregations, and forever drew the line between the established music of the city denominations and the smaller rural denominations.

The next giant step in gospel music's evolution came in 1877 in Singer's Glen, Virginia, when Joseph Funk's grandson, Aldine Kieffer, published *The*

Christian Harp. Kieffer, after his return from the Civil War, continued his grandfather's publishing business with a brand new type of book. *The Christian Harp* was a shape note songbook which specialized in songs for Sunday Schools and revivals. The 100 songs on the 128 pages had been sifted from the ponderous oblong books of his predecessor's day or were written especially for this publication. The long, thick book now gave way to the tall, thin one for "special singing" and not meant to be used for formal church services or choir anthems.

Gospel music is often criticized as inferior to the classical and more complicated music forms. Gospel was never intended for candidacy as an art form. In the beginning, as we have seen, people sang the melodies that to them were most easily recognized and least difficult to remember. To these melodies were added the words of a simple and basic faith, and these folk hymns were sung with little change for over 100 years. Now this simple type of religious song evolved as composers turned out both words and music, and quickly many new songs were being printed and sung by the people.

Yet the major ingredient in writing these songs is the same today as it was in 1877—simplicity. They are tunes that once heard can be readily whistled and remembered. The lyrics tell a story, at once uncomplicated and relevant, and the combination of music and story produces a song that the people can enjoy singing, that they love to hear performed. Gospel music was never intended to replace or exclude any type of music, and certainly not any form of church music that the people employ or desire. It has never been suggested that you could fairly compare gospel music with the works of Brahms or Beethoven.

In every man and woman's heart there is a place for a song, and since few can hope to reproduce the genius of Mozart and Handel, a need exists for a music commensurate with everyday talents. In *White Spirituals In the Southern Uplands* by George Pullen Jackson, there is this observation: "This is democratic music making. All singers are peers. And the moment selection and exclusion enter, at that moment this singing of, for, and by the people loses its chief characteristic."

Gospel is a music of participation as much as or more than it is a spectator's music. While it is fine to sit and appreciate the performance of others, the tobacco farmer, the grocery clerk, and the mailman seek the opportunity to express themselves musically. Gospel gives them this chance by remaining on a non-classical, informal level, so that the least melodic throat can possess its notes and acquire a very personal ownership of each song.

Again from Jackson: "Their emotional catharsis was one hundred per cent. . . . the blessing of this music-making and the prime reason, perhaps for its longevity; a blessing which obviously cannot descend upon those ominously great masses of mere hearers of music."

This music is written for all people to sing, not composed for performance by fine artists alone. The professionals do present enjoyable programs structured on these tunes, but the original purpose for their existence is the singing at Pleasant Hill and Macedonia churches.

In the finest sense of the word, gospel is common music, meant for the common man and for his rendering of its song, a tune he can hum and words that express what he believes. Gospel music has given to all who want it, the song that fits their hearts and lips. For nearly 200 years its composers have provided us with the glad song of Zion.

★ ★ ★

Aldine Kieffer quickly adopted Jesse Aiken's notation system and began printing songbooks using it. This seven shape note system is now universally employed and was important because it bound the Southern singers into one mutually accepted method. Others soon began using Aiken's notations; William Walker in 1873 published *The Christian Harmony* with many new songs composed in the new style.

The songs in Kieffer's *Christian Harp* were different from the old folk hymns in several ways. They were now even more optomistic in outlook and joyous in philosophy. Unlike many of the old songs, the gospel tunes did not dwell on the grave and did not give death the emphasis it had received before. One old song written in Singer's Glen by a fasola composer had told the story of one of Joseph Funk's great nephews, who died in early childhood and prompted the lament of "The Little Grave on a Green, Green Hill." It was a doleful lamentation and, as was the common practice, was always sung in its entirety, even if that complete version included 17 verses.

But in the new gospel songs, greater stress was laid on this life with a positive view of what this life could be. There was still the hope and expectation of a heaven, but the message seemed to be, "Enjoy this world while you are here." Happiness permeates each song and the choruses are vibrant, almost victorious. The new songs were also unique in that they were written, both words and music, by one person and were composed exclusively for this publication. There was no longer the wedding of old melody to new lyrics; the whole song was individually composed. Also, these tunes were written totally in major keys, while many of the old folk hymns had been set in minor chords. The introduction of instrumental accompaniment was a factor which delighted the organists and pianists who now had an active part in the performance of these songs.

Ira D. Sankey (1840-1908) gave this music its name with his publication of *Gospel Hymns*, establishing that title as the generic term. In fact, in many areas of the foreign mission field, the natives refer to any gospel song as a "Sankey," due to their acquaintance with the missionary's Sankey songbook.

Lang, in *One Hundred Years of Music in America*, makes this statement: "From Cairo to Honolulu, and from Sao Paulo to Madras, American evangelical missionaries have so thoroughly imbued converts with this kind of song that 'gospel' music now dominates nearly every foreign language hymnal. The proof of how quickly this kind of music has won friends in alien fields can be found in even such a book as *Standard Buddhist Gathas and Services*...the English language section of which is filled with 'a body of good, worthy hymns and services' that would do credit to a Homer E. Rodeheaver collection. Even in Europe, gospel hymnody has not lacked its advocates."

Among other composers contributing in these early days of gospel was Philip P. Bliss (1838-1876), a student of William Bradbury. Bliss worked as music conductor for Dwight Moody and, a singer-evangelist in his own right, authored many gospel songs. Dr. William H. Doane (1832-1915) penned his first musical composition at the age of 16, became a very successful executive in the business world, but came back to his first love and published *Sabbath School Gems* in 1862. He was the author of about 2,300 songs and cantatas and is particularly remembered for his Christmas cantatas. Altogether he published about 40 books which enjoyed a worldwide audience and were translated into every major language. In 1875 Denison University conferred upon him the title of Doctor of Music. His death came at the age of 83.

Even before the publication of *Christian Harp,* Kieffer was busy in the gospel music field. In 1870 he had begun printing *The Musical Million,* a monthly periodical devoted to rural music, singing schools and their teachers, and songs and songbooks in shaped notes. Published for 40 years, this paper unified the Southern devotees of shape note music. Kieffer himself was often referred to as "The Don Quixote of Buckwheat Notes" due to his monthly editorial page in *The Musical Million,* in which he frequently attacked the "roundheads" or adherents of conventional notation. He favored rural over urban music and expressed often his affinity for congregational singing as opposed to the paid choirs and salaried soloists found in the big city churches. With his brother-in-law, Ephraim Ruebush, Kieffer in 1872 established the publishing company of Ruebush-Kieffer in Dayton, Virginia, which exists today as the Shenandoah Press and is headed by a descendant, James Ruebush.

The Musical Million carried the circuits and the successes of the traveling singing teachers. Well-attended conventions and large, multi-pupiled schools were reported as news for the subscribers and encouragement for the other teachers on the road. Knowing of the scorn of the sophisticated city musician toward gospel's elementary techniques, Kieffer strived to sustain the dignity and uphold the merit of the religious country music. His paper was blatant propaganda, supportive of the shape note music and its instructors; and those who rode astride and clopped down dusty paths to the next village of singing enthusiasts appreciated his heartening and emboldening words and messages.

Aldine Kieffer's dream was the building of a normal school of music to provide better trained and more musically educated teachers for the singing schools. Finally, in August 1874, in the Shenandoah Valley, the Virginia Normal School of Music opened its doors with B. C. Unseld as its principal. Unseld was a subscriber to the standard round note system, so in compromise with Kieffer, both note systems were taught in the school. But this did not prove to be a practical solution; there was too much conflict between the two methods. Kieffer won out, and only the shaped notes were then taught. From this institution came the leaders who were to establish publishing companies, write songs, conduct singing classes, and very importantly, to train the next generation's teachers. Its graduates went to nearly every state and section of the South, teaching in and even establishing several new normal schools. George Pullen Jackson comments on the far-reaching effects of the Virginia Normal School: "There has been hardly a singing-school teacher of any standing in the entire Southern shape-note field during the past four or five decades [this written about 1932] who cannot trace his music-educational inspiration directly or indirectly to the Shenandoah Valley normal schools." A few of the more notable alumni were J. D. Vaughan and A. J. and J. A. Showalter. The Virginia Normal School is still in operation, but today teaches the classics and endorses the round notes which Kieffer so despised.

Gospel music is now an entity, entire unto itself. It is young and alive and lusty; yet, in its notes you can still hear 150 years of a people's love and devotion.

Chapter 4
Singing in the Southern Highlands

Beginning in the eighteenth century two breeds of pioneers climbed the Appalachian Mountains and parted pine boughs to look down into the fertile, blue valleys. The Mennonite and the Scotch-Irish settlers of the Southern Highlands shared an affinity for thrift, industrous living, and a religiously inspired lifestyle. Each exhibited a pragmatism developed by past experiences and present life-sustaining needs.

The folk of German and Dutch descent, from a more rigorous oppression in Europe, feared and despised any hint or suggestion of the military which had persecuted and harassed the Anabaptists. Consequently, both the Mennonite and the Amish eschewed any trappings of a martial world and accepted only clothing made without soldier's buttons and metal fasteners. The men relied on suspenders for trouser support, while the women donned severe dresses covered with white aprons, and wore the stiff white caps which satisfied hygienic requirements in their kitchens and covered long braids which might otherwise have become a temptation of vanity.

Stress was, and is, placed on frugality, simplicity, and hard work. Many of the Mennonite and the Amish later chose to refuse the innovations of technocracy and retained homes devoid of electricity, machination, and even modern plumbing. But their strength was always evident in their family units. Believing contraception a sin, they accepted birth as a gift from God, doted on their children, but disciplined them with an iron hand. This combination of love and restriction produced a segment of our society in which juvenile delinquency and civil disorder were, and remain, non-existent. Alcohol and tobacco were of course, prohibited, and the people emerged as healthy Americans who fought to win the right to school their children themselves and keep them from the educational institutions of the "English," as they referred to all people not of their sect, a practice still in existence.

Their pleasures and joys were found in their family experiences, their church life, and in the gratification of the harvests of their labors. Famous for their culinary talents, their tables were set with bounty—rich, delicious dishes originating from field and slaughterhouse, and spiced only with their back door herb gardens.

The hardy mountain settlers, who were predominantly Scotch-Irish, practiced the same principles of frugality and industriousness as did their German neighbors, but their necks had not felt an oppressor's iron collar, and so they came with a livelier step and with their fiddles slung over their backs. The bow string often reminisced of bagpipes and heather, but the tunes were melodious more than sad, and soon the highland notes swung into jigs and reels. Memories of potato famine and crop failure at times produced a dour Scotsman or a doleful Irishman, but the bottom land in the valleys was black and rich, and augured a brighter future. These settlers built homes, wedded their sons and daughters, and the resulting posterity was a mountain people who understood the value and necessity of a day's labor, but looked forward to the evening shindigs under the branches of the walnut trees and the stars.

Each of these pioneer groups of our Southern Highlands retained individual characteristics, but always shared the love of a God who felt quite close in either cornfield or rapid-swept river, and they worshipped Him in similar services of unsophisticated singing and basic Bible preaching.

Both ethnic groups greatly influenced and contributed to the perpetuation of American religious music. Joseph Funk, as has been noted, was originally a Mennonite, as was A. Henry Showalter. Funk's separation from the sect came mainly due to their aversion for musical instruments, which prohibited even piano and organ from their churches. This antipathy for instrumentation created song leaders who, from necessity, must have perfect pitch to guide the congregation through their hymns in a harmonious manner. Actually there were few churches of any denomination which employed musical instruments before the Civil War, either from reasons theological or from financial limitations. Consequently, in all Mennonite congregations, and in most other Protestant churches, the children received musical training, first on mama's knee, then, when old enough, as members of the youth choir.

Once or twice a week the children were brought to the church and taught to sing, following the vocal examples of the song leaders. They might display their new talents at a worship service from time to time, but for the most part, they sang at home with brothers and sisters while doing their chores. The result was that they, like their elders, could begin a song in any voice part compatible with their range, and in perfect pitch. How beautiful it is to sit in a Mennonite church and hear the men's and women's different parts sung in complete harmony. And they accomplish this feat without being sectionalized; an alto may be sitting with four sopranos, but she never misses or fluffs a note. In English or German, the results of a lifetime of voice coaching fill the square, frame churches with melodies of beauty and grace.

Singing in the Southern Highlands

Many of both the Mennonite and Scotch-Irish songsters were caught up in the excitement of the new gospel music, but the emergence of this new sound left behind the singers of the plainsong melodies. The fasola folk elected to stay musically as they were, and this is not to say that they were right or wrong. As it is a people's music, it is indeed the people's choice to suspend their song and protect it from the encroachments and influences of the modern world. Still, in parts of the South and the Southwest, the steadfast gather to join in the old bittersweet songs of the *Sacred Harp* and the *Christian Harmony*.

In Etowah schoolhouse in Henderson County, North Carolina, a *Christian Harmony* singing is held every six months. People come from several states with dinner baskets and intentions to stay until the last note is sung. There are many grayed ladies who still adhere to the highly starched, long-sleeved dresses of modesty, which show only a small amount of cotton stocking disappearing into black, laced oxfords. They have come with husbands whose bifocals and brown spots belie their age, while their leathered skin and reddened complexion attest to their lifetime of work. There are many young people, too, though not as many perhaps as the old singers would like, for they fear that their music is dying out. Still several sons and daughters come, and an increasing number of college students interested in a musical history that is still alive.

The singings are conducted as they have always been. Preference now dictates the avoidance of instruments. Each adult present, if he or she desires, is called upon to lead a song. All have brought their personal copies of the oblong *Harmony;* some of the books had been first used by their grandparents, and are treasured family possessions. The songbooks are passed from one generation to the next, and often chronicle the family's genealogy on the back page in nowfaded ink. The lovely old songs fill the Sunday quiet, and many eyes never glance at the opened book held loosely on the lap, for the words have been retained and cherished and fall easily from the lips.

It would be sad if this music should ever be lost completely, and it is hoped that there will always be a handful of the faithful to nurture and sustain this segment of our musical heritage.

Part III
Growth and Development

Chapter 1
Vaughan: Progenitor and Predecessor

A precedent was set in 1877 when Kieffer and Ruebush published the first book comprised solely of gospel songs. A young boy of thirteen in Giles County, Tennessee, sang these songs and was so impressed that he began years of musical study and a lifetime of work in gospel music.

James D. Vaughan and his three brothers walked the country miles to attend singing schools, and James learned to sing with a voice so versatile that he could sing each of the four parts of harmony. In 1892 he and his brother Charles Wesley stepped into the Shenandoah Valley to study at the normal school which Kieffer had instigated and B. C. Unseld directed. Together they studied at yet another normal school under E. T. Hilderbrand, and always at James' side was this younger brother who worked for, and with, him until Charles Wesley's death in 1965.

One of the largest and most famous gospel publishing companies grew from this advanced study and ever-increasing love for and interest in the music. While still studying, Vaughan had taught singing schools and in the public school systems since the age of 18. Then in 1902, as the world turned to face 100 new years, Lawrenceburg, Tennessee, came to be the birth place of the J. D. Vaughan Publishing Company, which in the intervening years has printed well over 6,000,000 books, including textbooks and other teaching aids.

The Vaughan School of Music was opened in 1911, and earnest, young men with starched-up collars and slicked-down hair came to learn and to follow the example set by Vaughan himself, which was to go out and teach others.

The *Vaughan Family Visitor,* a monthly periodical, carried gospel news, messages, and lessons to thousands of people for 30 years. Beginning in 1919, Vaughan published a weekly paper, the *Lawrenceburg News,* which was circulated for 20 years. Becoming very active in civic affairs, he served at varying times on the city school board, the city council, and was, for a term, mayor of

Lawrenceburg. Charles Wesley, consistently his brother's aide, edited both the *Vaughan Family Visitor* and the *Lawrenceburg News,* and taught in the School of Music, managing the first quartet for 12 years. Charles also occupied the mayor's chair for several years and was a state senator of Tennessee, and later a state representative. On his ninetieth birthday in January of 1965, Charles Vaughan was named "Mr. Lawrence County"; he died three months later.

But of the many contributions that James D. Vaughan made in his field, the greatest and most far-reaching was his organization of the quartets which he put on the road to sing his songs and sell his books. A goodly number of these singers came from his school, and it is reputed that the idea of the quartet itself originated there. This cannot be substantiated, but it is a certainty that he was the first to put together these groups of four and send them to conventions and concerts as performers of the gospel song. Tom and Lena Speer, and others to become legends in the history of this music, first traveled the circuits of the Southern singings in automobiles which had to be cranked, watered with some regularity, and generally pampered, to induce them to bump out the miles for the small commission from the book sales and a love offering.

James D. Vaughan had visions, but it is doubtful that he foresaw the sons and daughters of these same people cruising the super highways and interstates in Silver Eagles.

The short-skirted Tennessee girls who were agog at Clara Bow and strived for cupid lips and spitcurls, and the husky young men who were still enjoying the novelty of cokes and the opportunity they presented for a go at masculinity if drunk with a match stick dangling from the corner of their mouths, were even more amazed with the new phenomenon of radio as Vaughan built WOAN and Tennessee had broadcasting for the first time. Certainly appliance stores must suddenly have begun including radios in their inventories—huge wooden boxes that miraculously produced a quartet singing a Vaughan song such as "I Feel Like Traveling On." WOAN exists now as WREC in Memphis, and different quartets fill the air time, but many of the songs are the same. One that had a resurge of popularity recently was another Vaughan composition, "I Dreamed I Searched Heaven For You."

A few groups were on the road independently at this time, the first being the LeFevres in 1921, but the Vaughan quartets were the first to be backed by a publishing house, and, as shall be seen, it was predominately these groups which endured and gave us such names in the business as Blackwood, Speer, and John Daniel—individuals who later left Vaughan to form groups of their own. The precedent set by James Vaughan, and the effect that it has had on the industry, is immeasurable. With a large company, well-known and of good repute, behind them, and with the song books to sell for a little cash in hand, the gospel singers took off in their Model T's and Chevies and crossed the state lines and met the people on the route that was destined to be the highroad that led into the tomorrow of a vast professionalized business.

Radio, as experienced by the founders of broadcasting, was a medium totally different from that of the present day. All programs were live, the invention of the tape recorder being in the future. The sound equipment was primitive, and certainly the early broadcasts were as tinny in their quality as were the first cylinder recordings. The quartet singers shared one microphone, and in later years when the gear became more sophisticated and each member had a mike of his own, the singers were very thankful to be freed from the squeezed position. The acoustical systems in the studios were not very sophisticated either, and that problem—combined with the necessity for mike sharing—caused some singers to belt out the songs at great volume in hopes of being heard. Naturally the strongest voice won the volume contest and the weakest lost many of his best notes in the harmony. The pianists were on their own, and did their best with runs and trills to get in a lick or two between chorus and verse. And since these programs were live, if someone booted a note or forgot his lyrics, there was nothing to do but carry on and hope that the mistake was not too obvious.

As radios came within the reach of the average family's pocketbook, the Tennessee hills soon resounded with melodies sung by such men as Jim Waites and Otis McCoy, who were to spend their lives singing the gospel and instilling in their listeners a fond remembrance that lingers yet.

The Vaughan Quartet was the first sacred quartet to sing on radio, and in that original group with his Uncle Charles, was Glen Kieffer Vaughan, James' son. He had studied under Unseld, George W. Sebren, and others, and now at 30 he sang what was then called second tenor (or lead) in this broadcasting first. He managed and sang in many other Vaughan quartets and worked as announcer and manager of WOAN. Under his leadership, some of these quartets made recordings which he distributed to the other stations then in operation. In 1935 he took one of the quartets to WSM in Nashville, where they were heard for four years. Upon his father's death, Glen Vaughan became joint owner of the company with his sister, Grace Walbert, running it until 1964.

Needless to say, with quartets on the highways and in the hedgerows, and singing every day on the radio, the publishing company rapidly began selling more and more books. Songs like those written by Adgar M. Pace—"That Glad Reunion Day," "I'll Ride on the Clouds," and "I Can Tell You Now the Time"—were hummed and enjoyed by the listeners who determined to get a book so they, too, could learn to sing them.

Adgar M. Pace looked up from his work one day in the cotton field. Sweat ran into his eyes as he gazed into the fiery Georgia sun, but he felt that he saw most clearly and heard most distinctly, within himself, the insistent voice that urged him toward a pilgrim's journey. Such was his faith, that he laid down his hoe and, walking away, told his brothers that any who would, could have his fields and his home. Long since a singer, composer, and teacher of gospel songs, he chose the call of a lifetime of work which found him at its end as music editor for Vaughan Publishing Company. He was one of many men to join James Vaughan and to add his talents wherever they were needed. Although a writer of songs himself, he also edited and arranged songbooks for the company. The National Singing Convention was organized by him, and he served as its first president.

A point that is notable about Adgar Pace, and one which was true of almost all the men who walked the first miles of professional gospel, and who are honored in its Hall of Fame, is that they never ceased in their instruction of others. Even in his twilight years, Adgar Pace's strong bass voice could be heard leading congregations at Mountain Page Church in North Carolina or in countless other small churches across the gaps and gorges of the Appalachian Mountains. Only his death in 1959, at age 77, stilled the voice that sang the song he heard that day so long ago as he had stood on red clay soil and had dreamed of "riding on the clouds."

The people bought the books, joyfully harmonized through the choruses, and never forgot the songs. Many of these tunes are still sung, but even the ones that have been overlooked for some years have been preserved by the older gentleman who owns the service station on the corner, by the wife of the tobacco planter, and by the aunt who still comes to church on Homecoming Day in her Sunday best—the starched cotton print dress, long at the wrists and the ankles and high to the throat, adorned only with her mother's brooch. Sitting square on her head is the black straw sailor's hat, kept firmly in place by pearl-knobbed hat pins. And as for the cotton stockings—well, everyone knows that nylon not only clearly reveals the leg, but also runs and is highly impractical.

But the old songs are safely stored in their minds and in trunks in the attic's alcove. The love for them has never diminished, and while auntie would never show her calf, she has no hesitation in displaying a great enthusiasm for the singing after the Homecoming dinner. Tears of joy, and sometimes, if a very old melody is sung, tears of memory, slip down her cheeks: memories of when he was still alive and the children were little, running and playing behind the wood box as she was frying the supper's sidemeat and potatoes. The radio carried over the laughter and the sizzle of the frying pan with the songs of hope and cheer which she loved and came to cherish, and which have been so integrated with her life that memory overlaps into memory, and for her, it has been good.

At Mr. Ward's Gulf station you can still hear the radio playing inside, and while Elmer Cole's "Ten Thousand Years" doesn't sound very much like "Angel Band," Jonas Ward has grown with gospel music and has enjoyed each change of style. However, stacked on a shelf near his desk are many of the old books from which the Vaughan quartets first sang, and Jonas hasn't forgotten any of those songs. In fact, at the slightest invitation he will sing one for you, remembering well the melody and the meter. His patrons sometimes go in and sit in the string-bottomed chair and listen as he reminisces of the old days and the way "Big Jim" Waites could sing bass. He and many others hold the opinion that bass singers who gained a measure of fame and success had attempted to copy the style of Waites, who sang for many years in Vaughan quartets.

James Vaughan's grandfather was born on a ship while his family was emigrating from Ireland. They settled in Tennessee, and the hardy Irishman built a water mill on Shannon's Creek which is still in use. This penchant for building that which will endure seems to run through each generation, for certainly James D. Vaughan built foundations for his music which his followers found sturdy enough to support tremendous growth and expansion. The contributions of his son, Glen Kieffer, will be discussed later. It is understandable why James Vaughan is remembered not just as a publisher or composer, but also as a teacher, for it is said that he could, with clarity, impart to others that which he knew. The year of his death was 1941, but the years of his memory continue.

Chapter 2
Stamps-Baxter: The Publishing Dynasties

It is almost impossible to categorize the men who made significant contributions to gospel music in the first half of the twentieth century. Almost all of them were composers (Vaughan himself having written 500 songs), most of them were teachers, quite a few were publishers, and many were performers. But for the sake of clarity, an attempt will be made to classify these men whose talents overlapped, and many of whom now are honored in the Gospel Music Hall of Fame. Since the music publishers, in many instances, paved the way, their story is at the forefront of gospel's launching into this century.

V. O. Stamps

Texas in 1892 was still a rough and tough country, and Virgil Oliver Stamps, son of a sawmilling man, soon developed strong muscles from hauling pulpwood. He used his hard-earned wages to buy every gospel songbook he could find, and finally in 1907 was able to attend his first singing school under R. M. Morgan.

When his father changed trades and bought a little store in Upshure County, Virgil worked there until 1914; simultaneously, he was teaching church schools. He possessed a rich bass voice and a strong personality with which he held his students' attention.

Then the resolution came for a life devoted to work in gospel music. During the next ten years he worked for the Tennessee Music Company, for Samuel W. Beazley, and for J. D. Vaughan. The year 1924 saw the birth of the V. O. Stamps Music Co., and that year Stamps published his first songbook, *Harbor Bells*, titled from one of his favorite songs.

At this time the V. O. Stamps School of Music held its first session, and on its faculty were men of stature in the field: Thomas Benton, C. C. Stafford, R. B. Vaughan, and Otis Deaton.

J. R. Baxter joined Stamps two years later, and there soon emerged the Stamps-Baxter Music Co. Now a huge concern, they advertise themselves as the largest music company in the world that deals solely with gospel music. The first year of the depression saw the main offices move to Dallas, Texas, where they remain today, along with branches in Chattanooga, Tennessee, and Pangburn, Arkansas. Soon after the company was established, Stamps organized his personal quartet in which he sang bass, a foursome that quickly became a favorite. Many other quartets were formed and trained in the school, so V. O.

called his personal group "The Old Original Quartet" to distinguish it from the rest.

One of this man's greatest accomplishments was his utilization of radio, and at one time he had 100 representative quartets on radio stations in various states, some on nationwide broadcasts. At the Texas Centennial Exposition of 1936, the singing of the original Stamps quartet on KRLD brought such a response that the station gave them a regular daily show which was estimated to have reached nine million people each day.

Virgil O. Stamps promoted the first all-night singing convention in Dallas, and such events have continued under the direction of his brother Frank. Songs written by Virgil include: "Love Is the Key," "Singing on My Way," and "I Am Going."

Publisher, composer, teacher, singer, and promoter—V. O. Stamps—the sawmiller's son from the backwoods of East Texas, died in 1940, leaving a name and a legacy that will always be synonymous with gospel music.

Frank Stamps: Memories by Glen Payne

Frank Stamps worked with his brother V. O. and taught in the Stamps Quartet School of Music for many years. He influenced and guided many young singers before his death in 1965.

Glen Payne, manager and singer for the Cathedral Quartet, has expressed a personal indebtedness and a lingering affection for Frank and Virgil Stamps. A Texas boy growing up in the thirties whose family had a very limited income, but who loved gospel music, had quite a problem as far as education was concerned. But when Glen Payne was 13, his grandmother decided that the depression's poverty carried with it no shame, and promptly wrote to V. O. Stamps directly, explaining Glen's desires and financial limitations.

The positive reply came with celerity; Payne was to attend the Stamps School of Music at no charge. Thus began four years of study under V. O., but more closely, Frank Stamps. Quartets were formed in the school for practice singing, and, at one time, Payne and Hovie Lister, who was later to form the Statesmen Quartet, harmonized together. This was one of numerous friendships which was to endure through the years.

Frank Stamps had been watching Glen Payne, and listening to him. He called him aside one day and made him a promise that when he graduated from high school there would be a job waiting for him. So in 1944, at the age of 17, Payne commenced his years with the Stamps Quartet, and to his immense thrill, sang in the same group with Frank Stamps.

Glen Payne soon discovered that a performer's life was about one percent glamor and 99 percent plain hard work. Traveling in cars, the quartet went somewhere almost every night for a concert or a convention. But no matter how many miles they had covered or what time they had returned to Dallas, every morning they had to be at the radio station for the 6:30 a.m. broadcast. Singing in the early part of the day is always more difficult than in the evening, but after riding nearly all night in a cramped-up sedan which offered little opportunity for sleep, the 6:30 broadcasts were downright painful. The singers transposed the songs way down low and just cut out the notes that they knew nobody could hit before breakfast. But it was a very popular show, receiving mail from all 48 states, and in the winter when the signal went across the border, they heard from Canadians as well. There were no wasted hours; afternoons were spent working in the print shop at the publishing house.

Glen Payne recalls the personal interest Frank Stamps took in those who worked for him. Some very sound advice was passed on by that gentleman, much of which, to a youngster in his teens who thought he had the world by the tail, came across as rather corny. But Payne respected Stamps and never forgot what one generation said to the next, and as his own life progressed, he found that everything the old man had said was true. In all probability, Payne could now be caught telling the new kids in the business, "Live what you sing."

Glen Payne remembers some firsts accomplished by the Stamps name. In 1927 the Stamps All-Star Quartet was the first gospel group to record on the RCA Victor label. Their pianist, Dwight Brock, Lena Speer's brother, had a first of his own. Brock initiated what is called the "turn around" in gospel music, designating the period after a group has finished verse and chorus and before they begin the next verse. Prior to this time, the lapse between the chorus and the next verse had been filled by the pianist with a simple play-through of the verse to come, but now chorus back to verse could be turned around with music which set a mood and tempo either upbeat or downbeat. This was the instrumentalist's solo. It gave the pianists a short chance to show off their virtuosity with whatever runs, trills, or complex technique they wished to use. Dwight Brock went on in the business to retire in 1974 as president of Stamps-Baxter Music Co.

Payne remembers radio broadcasts when one, or sometimes two, mikes were used, and also concerts when there were no mikes at all and the singers had to rely on their own lung projection plus the quiet cooperation of the audience. He believes that a Stamps Quartet was one of the first to have a daily telecast, live in 1951 and in Dallas. At noon they did a radio show, and at 12:30 p.m. walked across the hall for the television show which was aired for one year.

Admitting that it is most assuredly much easier now than in those beginning days, Glen Payne (although still a young man of 50 but of the parent generation in gospel music) feels that the voice study and experience which were afforded him taught him how to take care of his voice, and he has no plans for retirement. He, along with others, expresses concern that young people in the field today do not seem to have any interest in concentrated musical study; for he too believes that you must first learn and then teach.

The Cathedral Quartet, under Glen Payne's leadership, has produced some milestones. They were the first group to record with strings and brass, and the first to go to the Holy Land and Hawaii on concert tours.

Payne's personal philosophy is that a song can sometimes reach a person who refuses to respond to the spoken word. For him gospel music is a ministry, and of his feelings toward the other people in his business: "I may not always agree with them, but I love them." Do the shadows of Frank and V. O. Stamps linger still?

★ ★ ★

There were many fine teachers in the Stamps School, and most of them were also composers. E. H. Wright, in his short lifetime of 36 years, not only taught but wrote such beloved songs as "Rocked on the Deep," "When the Shadows Roll Away," and "Sunset Is Coming, But the Sunrise We'll See." One verse and chorus of the latter song follows:

> Pilgrims for Jesus in a low-land of sin,
> Hoping that we at last a life crown may win.
> Serving the Master through the morning are we,
> Sunset is coming, but the sunrise we'll see.
>
> Sunset is coming, but the sunrise we'll see.
> Heavenly beauty makes the shadows to flee.
> Glory is waiting when the spirit is free.
> Sunset is coming, but the sunrise we'll see.

Bonanza, Texas, produced Otis Deaton, who was superintendent of the school in 1939 and 1940, instructed for many years, and composed 300 songs, one of which became the theme song for the Stamps Quartet and later for the original Blackwood Brothers Quartet. "Give the World a Smile" has done just that for over 40 years:

> Give the world a smile each day,
> Helping someone on life's way.
> From the paths of sin bring the wanderers in
> To the Master's fold to stay.
> Help to cheer the lone and sad,
> Help to make some pilgrim glad,
> Let your life so be that all the world may see
> The joy of serving Jesus with a smile.

Dan Cockerham organized the Stamps-Baxter Harmony Boys Quartet and wrote one of the most lovely songs to come from this period. "Love Will Roll the Clouds Away" is still sung and loved across the nation:

> As along life's way you go,
> Clouds may hide the light of day;
> Have no fear for, friend, you know,
> Love will roll the clouds away.
>
> Love will roll the clouds away,
> Turn the darkness into day;
> I'm so glad I now can say,
> Love will roll the clouds away.

James C. Coats' first song was published by Stamps-Baxter in 1933, and many more came after that, including "My Soul Shall Live On" and the continuing favorite, "Where Could I Go?":

Living below in this old sinful world,
Hardly a comfort can afford;
Striving alone to face temptations sore,
Where could I go but to the Lord?

Where could I go, O where could I go,
Seeking a refuge for my soul?
Needing a friend to save me in the end,
Where could I go, but to the Lord?

Lonnie and Myrtle Combs were in the original Stamps-Baxter Mixed Quartet, with Mrs. Combs singing alto and playing the accordian. The group broadcast over KRLD and WFAA and made several records.

An Alabama boy, Vernie O. Fossett became assistant editor of songbooks in 1939, and later editor-in-chief of the company. While singing tenor with the Baxter Quartet, he composed "Cross the Border Line" as well as many others.

★ ★ ★

J. R. Baxter, Jr.

Taught by T. B. Mosely and A. J. Showalter, J. R. Baxter showed such extraordinary teaching abilities that his instructors made engagements for him to conduct his own schools, even before J. R., or "Pap" as he affectionately came to be known, thought he was quite ready. He was considered by his teachers and by his peers alike to be unexcelled in the instruction of harmony.

But Showalter found it necessary to take Baxter from the teaching field to manage the Showalter Company, a position he held for several years. Then in 1926 he joined V. O. Stamps in that famous partnership and became president and general manager at the death of Stamps. He worked in this capacity for 23 years, also doing radio shows, teaching normal schools, and leading conventions. The Baxter Quartet was organized by him, and his personal radio program was "The Baxter Chorus."

Upon his death in 1960, his wife, Clarice or "Ma," who had worked with him through the years, assumed responsibility for the management of the company until her death a few years ago.

J. R. Baxter, Sr., watched as his son saw the Alabama sun for the first time in 1887. It would be interesting to know whether even in his wildest dreams for his young son, he could have conceived that someday this boy would become president of one of the largest gospel concerns in the world, would be a venerated teacher, and would become honored in the Gospel Music Hall of Fame.

A. J. Showalter

Showalter's father, John Anthony, was a contemporary of Kieffer and Unseld, and after his Dad taught him all he knew at home in Cherry Grove, Virginia, A. J. Went on to the Valley's Normal School, where he was taught by

Unseld. 1880 found him publishing books such as *Harmony and Composition* and *The Singing Tribute,* the first books of their kind by a Southern author.

The A. J. Showalter Publishing Co. was founded in Dalton, Georgia, in 1884, and the 60 books that were published sold into millions. Showalter established the Southern Normal Music Institute, which held sessions in several states. In 1905, he was the first to direct an all-day singing as part of the state fair in Atlanta. Probably the most famous song written by him was "Leaning on the Everlasting Arms":

> What a fellowship, what a joy divine,
> Leaning on the everlasting arms!
> What a blessedness, what a peace is mine,
> Leaning on the everlasting arms!
>
> Leaning, leaning,
> Safe and secure from all alarms;
> Leaning, leaning,
> Leaning on the everlasting arms!

Gospel music was his life from his antebellum birth in 1858, and inspired by great men, he lived to inspire others.

Upon Showalter's death, Thomas Benjamin Mosely became editor-in-chief of the company. He had served for 30 years as associate editor, after having been trained by A. J. himself. A composer and teacher, he had in 1910 organized in Alabama The Special School for Teachers, which had great influence over several Southern states. Showalter's life was an example of that which is seen everywhere in gospel music: teach others; pass on to the next generation that which they will need in order to instruct those who follow them.

John Benson

Another publishing company whose life began in the infancy of the twentieth century was that started in 1902 by John T. Benson. Two years later John T., Jr., was born to mature to manhood in Nashville, Tennessee, printing and distributing songbooks, sheet music, and records. Two record companies grew from this business, Heartwarming and Impact, both of which record many of today's top gospel singers.

Elmo Mercer worked for Benson, Jr., as editor of music and was the composer of "Each Step I Take" and "Nearer to Thee."

John Benson, Jr., retired in 1969, but John Benson III had long been working with his father, and was ready to assume leadership for the expanding concern established by his grandfather. Bob Benson, who had worked with the middle generation, now extends his influence on the third as well.

★ ★ ★

In the early 1900s, many cities of the Deep South which had felt Sherman's wrath, or had trembled in its repercussions, had now built back that which was ravaged, and had added to it structures, tall and bricked. Quite a few of these new buildings housed publishing companies in the new surge of printing gospel songs.

Ladies still carried parasols, screening their faces from the sun's tanning rays, and for a little extra insurance, used buttermilk to bleach cheeks pale. The sidewalks clicked with the jaunty step of the gentlemen in bowler hats and hand-ironed, detachable collars. The concrete tapped with the rhythm of the tips of the canes, carried more for effect than infirmity. Hightop, button shoes played hopscotch over the sidewalk's cracks, while knicker knees were worn thin shooting marbles; and alas the aggie that rolled from gutter to sewer.

Summertime brought out the town band for concerts in the city park. Canoe rides were romantic, and gas lights and the telephone, revolutionary.

The specter of war had not yet appeared, and men were determined to grow and extend themselves to whatever future they could envision. For if the country itself could span the continent and conquer the plains and deserts of the West, then they could certainly believe that now was the time of prosperity and a birthing era for careers unlimited.

Sweat shops and child labor still existed, but this was the day of social reform, these injustices would be corrected in due course. A few of the women began to moan and groan about, muttering suffrage and other such ribald ideas, but they, too, would come to their senses soon enough. The excitement, the euphoria of the dawning of the twentieth century was not to be denied, and men of dreams and determination launched their lives into the swelling and building wave that has continued its climb, and hasn't touched shore even yet.

★ ★ ★

In Atlanta, Georgia, Homer F. Morris and John M. Henson formed a music company which Henson bought out and ran as J. M. Henson Music until 1961, when it was sold to the Statesmen Quartet. Both Morris and Henson were students of A. J. Showalter and taught and composed most of their lives.

Oren A. Parris established the Parris Music Co. in Jasper, Alabama. With John Denson he revised the *Original Sacred Harp* and the *Christian Harmony.* In 1963 he organized the Convention Music Co. "Where the Shades of Love Lie Deep" was the most popular of Parris' compositions.

Harkins Freye, a West Virginia boy, was to work eventually and compose for Parris, but first published *Celestial Joy,* and in 1920 started Revival Music Co. In the early forties, he joined Oren A. Parris and wrote the popular songs "Time Has Made a Change in Me" and "Heaven on My Mind."

An Oklahoma Sooner, John Alexander McClung studied under Homer Rodeheaver and W. M. Ramsey, and began singing when he was 13 years old. He was president and owner of Hartford Music Co. and Hartford Musical Institute, and during his life composed such classics as "Standing Outside" and "Jesus the Rock."

Just before his death in 1942, he wrote "Just a Rose Will Do." This song is a favorite with soloists, and apparently is indicative of Mr. McClung's personal philosophy which he wished to convey before his own demise:

When I have come for my leaving,
When I bid you adieu;
Don't spend your money for flowers,
Just one rose will do.

I'll be the harmonization,
Just awaken to do;
Just have some old fashioned singing,
Just one rose will do.

Because I'm going to a beautiful garden,
That blooms when life's singing, it is all through;
Don't spend your money for flowers,
Just one rose will do.

Floyd Earl Hunter, a graduate of Eureka Conservatory of Music, began broadcasting over KTHS with the Hunter Quartet in that station's first years. Altogether, he logged over 31 years of air time over various stations. At the death of John McClung, Hunter became owner and editor of Hartford Music. A teacher and composer, he wrote: "One Wonderful Day," "Oh, What a Day," and "Way Down Deep in My Soul." "Way Down Deep in My Soul" was enthusiastically received by the quartets because it gave them a wide range of flexibility in using different voice parts in repeats and syncopation. The song itself had a fast tempo, and the men loved to get as many words into the music available as was possible. This arrangement was used with successful results by the Blackwood Brothers Quartet.

I have a feeling in my soul,
Since the Savior made me whole;
Way down, way down, *(tenor)*
A...way down deep in my soul. *(bass)*—"my soul"

I'm trusting Jesus every day,
For I know I'm on my way:
Way down, way down, *(bass)*
Yes, a....way down deep in my soul. *(bass)* "my soul"

Down in my soul, *(tenor)* *(remaining three)* "my soul"
I sing and pray, *(tenor)* *repeat* "and pray"
Till Christ shall come, *(tenor)* *repeat* "shall come"
To take me with him to stay *(tenor)* *(remaining three)* "to stay"
Then I'll be going to that home,
Never more from Him to ro....am. *All sing and stretch out* "roam"
Way down, way down, *(bass)*
Yes, a....way down deep in my soul. *(bass)* "my soul"

The light of heaven, I now can see,
For He came and set me free:
Way down, way down, *(tenor)*
A....way down deep in my soul. *lead voice one key higher than others*

I know there's glory to behold,
For I feel it in my soul; *lead voice is above others*
Way down, way down *(bass)*
A. . . . way down deep in my soul.

Singing now more slowly:
Down in my soul I'll sing and pray,
Till Christ shall come to take me with Him to stay;
Then I'll be going to that home,
Never more from Him to roam.
Way down, way down *(bass—going for his lowest note)*
Then faster:
Yes, a. . . . way down deep in my soul.

This is only one arrangement of the many possible for this and all the gospel songs which contained a great deal of maneuverability. The change in tempo, in voice part lead, and the repetition of the phrases made the songs more interesting for the listeners, and more fun for the singers.

At the turn of the century, there were many small companies independently owned by men who published, edited, composed, and taught. T. R. Sisk, Sr., created Sisk Music in Georgia, while W. M. Ramsey established Central Music Company in Little Rock, Arkansas. Robert and Cora Arnold, who sang at one time with the Central Music Quartet, taught 300 singing schools, wrote "No Tears in Heaven," and owned and operated National Music in Jefferson, Texas.

Oliver and Evie Boone operated the Convention Music Company in Montgomery, Alabama, and wrote "I'm a Happy Pilgrim." M. Lynwood Smith, who worked for the Boones' printing house, penned "I'm Going Home."

In the North, Praise Publishing Company was started by William J. Kirkpatrick. In 1878, he and John R. Sweney compiled 49 songbooks which sold into the millions. Sweney, a child prodigy, was teaching music before the battles of the North and South demanded his attention. The post-war years found him professor of music at Pennsylvania Military Academy for 25 years and recipient of a Doctor of Music degree in 1886. He created many anthems and cantatas, but the composition for which he is probably best remembered is "Beulah Land":

I've reached the land of corn and wine,
And all its riches freely mine;
Here shines undimmed one blissful day,
For all my night has passed away.

My Savior comes and walks with me,
And sweet communion here have we;
He gently leads me by the hand,
For this is heaven's borderland.

Chorus

O Beulah Land, sweet Beulah Land,
As on thy highest mount I stand,
I look away across the sea,
Where mansions are prepared for me,
And view the shining glory shore,
My heav'n, my home forevermore!

Chapter 3
The Composers

Many gospel songs have been written over the years: some endure, many are transient, a few have become classics which are sung and loved as much today as when they were first written. These enduring hymns adhere to the criteria for a gospel song: they are simple in style and lyric, and they tell a story.

One man has probably written more of these gospel classics than any other. Albert E. Brumley sucked in his first lungful of Oklahoma dust in 1905 and remains with us today, legend and man. Bare toes digging into LeFlore County dirt, he chopped cotton and fought the weevil while singing to himself the gospel tunes that would someday be translated into four languages and braille.

Age 17 saw him begin his musical studies, instructed by Rodeheaver, Benton, Ruebush, Bartlett, Stamps, and at the Hartford Music Institute. The study and instruction were necessary, but it was surely from his soul that came the 600 songs he was to write.

Prolific, yes, but each song carries its own special flavor, and Brumley has given to us songs in various styles: "I'll Fly Away," "Jesus, Hold My Hand," "If We Never Meet Again," and "I'm Bound For That City."

I'll Fly Away

Some glad morning when this life is o'er,
I'll fly away;
To a home on God's celestial shore,
I'll fly away.

When the shadows of this life have grown,
I'll fly away;
Like a bird from prison bars have flown,
I'll fly away.

Chorus

I'll fly away, O glory,
I'll fly away;   in the morning *(bass line)*
When I die, Hallelujah, by and by,
I'll fly away.

This song, written in 1932, has been sung by churches and professional groups continually through the years. The whole song, but particularly the chorus, gives plenty of room for improvisations.

Albert Brumley wrote "Jesus, Hold my Hand" in 1933, then in 1936 he wrote the song that James Blackwood uses as his personal song of testimony, "I'll Meet You in the Morning." This song is beautiful when performed by someone of Blackwood's talents, but, more important, since it complies with the gospel standard of simplicity, the people themselves can sing its promise and joy. Sharing its words of hope and solace, the members of Bear Run and Piney Grove churches can look forward to that day when they can "auld acquaintance renew" with loved ones and friends that have already gone.

Like most men of his time and circumstance, Brumley took his knowledge, his music, and his message to the singing schools, and attempted to give to others from his own bounty. He wrote for Stamps-Baxter, then he and his five sons established two publishing houses in Powell, Mississippi, and gained control of the Hartford Music Co. His songs have been recorded by every performer in the field, and tribute albums of Brumley music have been cut by the Blackwoods, the Statesmen, the Chuck Wagon Gang, and several other groups. The songs of Albert E. Brumley, a member of Gospel's Hall of Fame, will be sung wherever and whenever the gospel note is struck.

★ ★ ★

The talents of these men in gospel's history overlap to such an extent that it is difficult to say that this one was noted as a teacher primarily, or that one a composer. They sang the music because they loved it, they wrote it because they felt it and were capable of expressing that emotion in song, and they taught because it was the heritage and method of necessity to instruct youth in order to propagate the life of the music.

Robert E. Winsett was one of the men whose talents grew tall to complement each other. This Tennessee gentleman lived from 1876 to 1952 and taught for 42 years. He wrote his first song at age seven, and in 1903 published his first book, *Winsett's Favorite Songs and Pentecostal Power Complete,* which sold into the millions.

His company, begun in 1929, was first located in Chattanooga, but was later moved to Dayton, Tennessee. Winsett printed over 67 songbooks and wrote more than 1,000 songs. His compositions include "Lift Me Up Above the

Shadows," "When I Reach That City," and "Jesus Is Coming Soon," which, after a revival of popularity, received the award as Gospel Song of the Year in 1969. One quartet got their start in popularity as they and almost every major group recorded the song in that year.

Jesus is Coming Soon

Troublesome times are here, filling men's hearts with fear,
Freedom we all hold dear now is at stake;
Humbling your heart to God saves from the chast'ning rod,
Seek the way pilgrims trod, Christians awake.

Troubles will soon be o'er, happy forevermore,
When we meet on that shore, free from all care;
Rising up in the sky, telling this world goodbye,
Homeward we then will fly, glory to share.

Chorus

Jesus is coming soon, morning or night or noon,
Many will meet their doom,
Trumpets will sound;
All of the dead shall rise,
Righteous meet in the skies,
Going where no one dies,
Heavenward bound.

Robert E. Winsett is honored in the Gospel Music Hall of Fame.

Luther Presley studied under J. H. Ruebush, and in 1907 published his first song, "Gladly Sing." Of the 1,500 songs composed by Presley, "I'd Rather Have Jesus" and "I'll Have a New Life" are two of his best and are often included on recordings today. Presley was inspired one Easter to write this song:

I'll Have a New Life

On the resurrection morning when all the dead in Christ shall rise,
I'll have a new body, praise the Lord, I'll have a new life;   eternal
Sown in weakness, raised in power, ready to live in Paradise,
I'll have a new body, praise the Lord, I'll have a new life.

I'll have a new home, glory, glory! Where the redeemed shall ever stand;
There'll be no more sorrow, no more pain, no more strife;
Raised in the likeness of my Savior, ready to live in Paradise;
I'll have a new body, praise the Lord, I'll have a new life.

What a hallelujah morning when the last trump of God shall sound,
I'll have a new body, praise the Lord, I'll have a new life.

Graves all bursting, saints all shouting, heavenly beauty all around;
I'll have a new body, praise the Lord, I'll have a new life;
I'll have a new home, glory, glory! Where the redeemed shall ever stand;
I'll have a new body, praise the Lord, I'll have a new life.

E. M. Bartlett, a contemporary of Presley, also studied under Ruebush, then earned his A. E., B. S., B. O., and Bachelor of Music degrees. Bartlett taught in public schools and served for a time as president of a college, but through the years was active in quartet work, conducted many singing schools, and was associated with various music companies. A composer of merit, he left us "Victory in Jesus," "Just a Little While," and "Everybody Will Be Happy Over There."

Everybody Will Be Happy Over There

There's a happy land of promise over in the great beyond,
Where the saved of earth shall soon their glory share;
Where the souls of men shall enter and live on forevermore,
Everybody will be happy over there.

There we'll meet the one who saved us and who kept us by His grace
And who brought us to that land so bright and fair;
Where we'll praise His name forever as we look upon His face,
Everybody will be happy over there.

Chorus

Everybody will be happy, will be happy over there,
We will shout and sing His praise,
Everybody will be happy over there.

A name that goes back even farther is George Cole Stebbins. A New York boy who moved to Chicago in 1869 at the age of 23, he worked for the major part of his life with Moody and Sankey, traveling the world with them. He organized the choirs for each of their crusades and edited the hymn books used at their meetings. He was also a soloist and often sang one of his own compositions, such as "There is a Green Hill Far Away" or "Saved by Grace."

In 1947 a farm boy from Alabama, Bobby Jean Burnett, met another farm lad, Videt Polk, coming from Pearl River, Louisiana, to attend the Stamps-Baxter School of Music in Dallas. They formed a friendship and a writing partnership at the same time. In 1956 they organized the Gospel Singers of America School of Music, which trains and promotes gospel singers and writers. Polk continues to work for Stamps-Baxter as a field representative, but remains president of the school in Pass Christian, Mississippi, where Bobby Burnett and his wife are regular members of the teaching staff. Songs written by Burnett and Polk include "He Cares for You" and "My Lord Grows More Precious to Me."

The Kansas plains chilled at the touch of winter's foreboding winds in November 1921, but from the gust of those winds came the birth of John W. Peterson, the last of the seven born to his family. Just before the war, he and two of his brothers made the round of singings and for the sum of eight dollars sold his first song, "Yet There is Room."

Melodies seemed to come to him in unorthodox circumstances, and he wrote wherever he found himself. "It Took a Miracle" grew note by note as he flew a solo mission during World War II. After the war, he graduated from the American Conservatory of Music in Chicago. Among his songs are "Springs of Living Water," "So Send I You," and "Over the Sunset Mountain." John W. Peterson is head of Singspiration, Inc.

Many composers have written songs that will be sung for generations to come. They are too numerous to list, but a few are given here.

Ira S. Stanphill: "Mansion Over the Hilltop," "Supper Time," and "I Know Who Holds Tomorrow."

Eugene Horton Whitt: "As For Me and My House," "Crossing the Bar," "I'm Headed for the Promised Land."

Thomas W. Day: "Let It Fall on Me," "He Leadeth Me," "That Will Be Heaven For Me."

Joe E. Parks: "Some of These Days," "Empty Hands," "Wait Till You See Me In My New Home":

> Here on earth you talk and brag about all your wealth untold,
> About your silver and your gold;
> Mansions on display, homes in bright array, mock me as I roam,
> Just wait till you see my new home.
>
> You talk about your priceless jewels rich and rare,
> I praise the Lord for mansions bright beyond compare;
> So if you think you're a wonder, Earthly goods you may squander,
> Wait till you see me in my new home.
>
> If a mansion you own, while here on earth I now roam,
> Just wait till you see me in my new home;
> If a castle you're sporting, while the devil you're courting,
> Just wait till you see me in my new home.

Marvin P. Dalton: "Looking for a City" and "What a Savior."

Mosie Lister, a composer of both merit and fame, began his life in the flapper year of 1921, and grew up amid the tall, rich pines and deep red clay of Georgia. His father was a music teacher; his home, a house of song. He took advantage of Georgia's "endless acres of afternoon," of which Benet speaks, to listen, observe, and write. Formal education came at Georgia Middle College, wher he majored in English. Later he studied with Adgar Pace and Tom Speer, and finally completed specialized study at Tampa University in harmony, counterpoint, and arranging.

He began writing for gospel groups in the late 1940s and in 1948 was hired as the arranger for the Statesmen Quartet. In 1953 he founded the Mosie Lister Publications Company, which merged with Lillenas Publishing in 1969. He continues to write and is quite active in many areas of the gospel field. Some of his best remembered compositions are: "Till the Storm Passes By," "His Hand in Mine," "Where No One Stands Alone," "Then I Met the Master," and "How Long Has It Been."

How long has it been since you talked with the Lord,
And told Him your heart's hidden secrets?
How long since you prayed?
How long since you stayed
On your knees 'til the light shone through?
How long has it been since your mind felt at ease?
How long since your heart knew no burden?

Can you call Him your Friend?
How long has it been since you knew that He cared for you?

Chapter 4
From Mules to Model T's: The Singing Teachers

Throughout the history of gospel music's composers and publishers, the phrase "he was also a teacher" is reiterated. There follows an attempt to depict men who must be honored as masters in education. Active in most other facets of the field, their instructive influence brought hundreds of eager young students to realize the fruition of their dreams for their own places in gospel music.

A majority of song writers and publishers have in their biographies the comment, "He was a pupil of Homer Rodeheaver." Present and at work in the fledgling days of professional gospel, Rodeheaver lived from 1880 to 1955. Rodeheaver struck the souls and imaginations of everyone near him with such impact and vitality that they never forgot the lessons he gave both orally and by example.

He established his own school of evangelistic singing and was president of the Rodeheaver-Hall-Mack Publishing Co., but he came out to the people in the role of teacher and thus reached literally thousands of pupils in the singing schools. From 1909 until 1931, he led the music for Billy Sunday's meetings. Once in the Atlantic City Auditorium, his massive choir was composed of 62,000 people. Later he directed the singing for 85,000 at Chicago's Soldier's Field.

One of his own compositions, "Brighten the Corner Where You Are," was a favorite of the huge tent meetings. When KDKA radio in Pittsburgh began broadcasting in the early 1920s, Rodeheaver had his own gospel show, and performed many of his own songs, including "Somebody Cares."

Winona Lake, Indiana, was the base for his evangelistic works. He, of course, sang, authored books, edited hymn books, and was always ready for evangelistic community sings. Homer Rodeheaver lived and sang what he believed, and trusted that the torch of his faith would be relayed through succeeding generations by followers who cared as deeply as did he.

* * *

Although its true meaning has often been confused or misconstrued, "character" is defined in Webster's New Collegiate Dictionary (1961) as "the aggregate of distinctive qualities belonging to an individual; the stamp of individuality impressed by nature, education, or habit." If in the history of gospel music there has lived a character, it must surely be Lee Roy Abernathy. This man created firsts, acknowledged and promptly subdued challenges, and touched all points of his field with an abounding energy and a firm belief in his own success.

Seeing no reason to wait for his later years to commence his career, he began singing with his father's quartet at age five. Being a good Georgia boy, he progressed, and when he was 11, in 1924, his father's ATCO Quartet made its recording debut on RCA. The young Lee Roy's tenor never faltered. As was the customary practice, the quartet was given a flat rate of 50 dollars, no royalties. Lee Roy took his cut of the profits as the opportunity to buy his first pair of long pants.

The necessity which brought Lee Roy and his dad to the Canton, Georgia Textile Mill, created a conflict which resulted in the termination of school for him in the seventh grade. But the boy did not neglect his musical studies and was taught by some of the best: A. J. Showalter, Adgar Pace, and J. M. Henson, among others. Eventually he learned to play the piano, trumpet, drums, guitar, accordian, and organ. So after 12 hours in the cotton mill, Lee Roy Abernathy, enterpriser that he was, took his knowledge and went door to door around the mill village teaching piano for 25 cents a lesson.

This money was promptly put back into more lessons for himself in Atlanta. He grew up and at 19 married—who else?—the boss' daughter. The marriage endures to this day with Louise Abernathy being all these years a source of solace and support to her ever-active husband.

Abernathy went into gospel music full time, forming his own quartets: first, the Modern Mountaineers, which enjoyed years of success, then the Electrical Workers Quartet with "Big Jim" Waites singing bass. At 23 he moved to Dalton, Georgia, teaching in the public schools of Whitfield County and continuing his habit of traveling wherever he had to go to teach. He instructed in homes in Rome, Cedartown, and several other surrounding Georgia towns. When the itinerant was home long enough, he began arranging songs and writing lyrics. Although he had been on very familiar terms with ribbon lap machines and slubbers, he never let that minor distraction, or any other for that matter, veer him from his intended course.

Then the seeds for a new and unique method of teaching began to grow in his mind. In 1938 on WBLJ in Dalton, Abernathy introduced his "Radio School of Music." He had actually devised a way to teach piano by mail. Southerners raised on shape note music sent for his correspondence course and found that they could now play the gospel tunes they had so long been singing. The "Gospel Piano Course" was a revolutionary first.

The Singing Speer Family were contemporaries of Lee Roy Abernathy and made one of their first records at his studios in Dalton. The year after the war found him in Chattanooga playing piano for the Sand Mountain Boys and plugging his lessons. For a while he organized and sang with the Four Tones.

After playing for the Rangers a little over a year, he joined a quartet which was created by Connor Hall and which has become gospel legend. The Homeland Harmony Quartet included James McCoy, Shorty Bradford, and Aycel Soward. Successful at recording and on television in Atlanta, the group established the "Homeland Harmony Distributors." This venture involved getting their records into the department stores, five-and-ten variety stores, and jukeboxes where gospel records had never been handled or played before. At the time, only a few major labels could find shelf space in some record shops; this distribution service made available to many more people the records of gospel artists. The Homeland Harmony made prosperous use of one of Abernathy's songs, "Gospel Boogie," but as boogie fazed out, its title was changed to "Everybody's Going to Have a Wonderful Time Up There."

The Homeland disbanded, but a lasting and close relationship had been established between Lee Roy Abernathy and Shorty Bradford. For three years, the people from Maryville and Clinton could see "The Happy Two" appearing on Channel 6 in Knoxville, Tennessee. Cas Walker sold his groceries, the kids at the University of Tennessee strolled Cumberland Avenue, holding hands and visiting the malt shops, and a jeweler on Gay Street offered a 500 dollar diamond ring to anyone who could sing as high or as low as Shorty.

On the Georgia State Network daily for a year, they appeared with the LeFevres, Hovie Lister and the Statesmen, and many others. Shorty Bradford then organized another quartet in 1949, which they called The Miracle Men, with Abernathy, naturally, at the piano.

But first and ever, Lee Roy Abernathy has been a teacher. On every broadcast, at every opportunity over the years, he told the audiences about his home courses for musical study. Altogether he has taught over 100,000 people by mail, and his courses are still available and advertised in the trade papers of the field. Affectionately, he has been dubbed "professor," but the book which he published in 1947, *It,* containing songs and musical techniques, also held a very valuable lesson for the novice or naive songwriter. *It* gave a clear and concise explanation of how and why to copyright a song.

Professor Lee Roy Abernathy, the character who wasn't afraid to attempt the novel or the unusual, taught either in person or by mail many famous names in gospel music.

★ ★ ★

The hammerhead mule had been replaced by the Model T Ford which, on the bumpy roads, was perhaps a bit speedier, but didn't relieve the discomfort of the ride to an appreciable extent. The passenger still wiped the Deep South sweat and grit from his face with a huge pocket handkerchief and was forced to stop occasionally to drag from his path a log or boulder which had been swept down by a summer's sudden storm or a spring's torrent of rain.

In a cloth bag, he carried an extra white shirt, his Bible, comb, tablet, and pencil. If at the last church he had found generosity combined with culinary talent, he had his lunch wrapped in brown paper: ham biscuits, or in harder times, cornbread and a couple of green onions.

A cool spring or creek afforded dining space, something to drink, and an opportunity to wash up. Dipping his comb in the stream, he drew his hair back into place, put on the clean shirt, and if there had been a biscuit for lunch, he saved a small piece to polish his patent shoes. Minus a biscuit, a brushing with a black gum twig would have to suffice. Thus fortified and looking his best, the singing teacher was once again headed for his destination—the church or school over the next rise, and then the one in the lower end of the county, then across the state line where it became flatter, sandier, and the oases were much more scarce.

These men are legend now, but were flesh and blood fact in the earlier years of our century. The memory of these teachers lingers around the cleared ground where once stood a white frame church that has been replaced by a stolid brick building. Sometimes in those old churches that have been bricked-up, plastered over, re-windowed, fully carpeted, and even air conditioned, you can still feel the presence and vitality of those who once stood in the front, and with a vigorous right arm led the choir through a new song by singing the notes.

A Sunday night singing will still bring visiting ministers and singers from miles around. As they sit on the front pews, the older ones respond to an old song in varying ways. A smile flits across the corners and lines of a grandfather's face with remembrances of a youth standing as close as possible to the little alto in the lavender print dress who smelled of fresh sunshine and clean wood smoke. The two harmonized as L. D. Huffstutler led the school in one of his songs, "Deep Down in My Soul."

The man who, from the necessity of work at an early age, still cannot read or write his own name, learned from Sam Beazley his songs by first listening and then with quick retention, beginning to sing with the rest, "Jesus Paid It All" and "Crossing the Bar." Singing teachers were never shy or retiring, and always between songs took the chance to tell the people of their own personal testimony and conviction. A number yet live who can recall Adgar Pace describing his own moment of conviction and confirmation before he sang, "I can tell you now the time, I can take you to the place, where the Lord saved me by His marvelous grace."

Many of today's youth are unaware of these masters of days gone by, and yet, if they asked, they would probably find that at least one of these teachers had touched the lives of their father or their father's father before him.

But the music of these men is interred in the tap roots of the white oak and the poplar which have grown tall since those melodies drifted to them through open windows. The pine and the palmetto sway with the wind, cradling the songs on sky-stretched branches. Down the mountain ridges, across the piedmont, through the swamps, Delta, dust bowls, and tidewaters came these teachers and their music. Many are gone now, many of those who heard are gone also, but the notes are captured by memory's web into the grass and rock, into the very land itself, and if it is never heard quite this same way again, it will not be dead, for it touched the earth and became part of it, and the earth does not die.

* * *

Throughout the South, the singing teachers took their knowledge into the smallest settlements and communities. Even the Cherokee Indians living on the Qualla Boundary in the Smoky Mountains of North Carolina were not neglected musically. William Walker Combs, born a Georgia cracker in 1883, went to his first normal school in 1906, and at the onset of war in 1914, traveled to J. D. Vaughan's School of Music and began a lifetime career of teaching. From 1918 until 1920, he lived on the Cherokee reservation and trekked up Panther Creek, Deep Creek, and into six counties, taking the gospel songs to a people long-since Christian, and longer still, lovers of music and free expression in their religion.

L. D. Huffstutler and John Daniel Williams were contemporaries of Combs and natives of Alabama. Huffstutler went on to teach for 20 years at the Stamps Conservatory of Music, but Williams, after completing his education, went back to Alabama and taught in the churches and also in the public schools, serving for a time as county superintendent in Monroe County. He organized and managed the Happy Hitters Quartet which sang over WBRC in Birmingham for 30 years. He was also the originator of the Song Festival of the South, the first all-night singing held in the city auditorium in Birmingham.

Williams was responsible for the program, "Grand Old Singing Convention Of the Air," which was broadcast on WBRC each Sunday morning for many years. He wrote over 50 songs, among them "God Will Make a Way for Me."

Another Alabama boy, born in the last years of the nineteenth century, was C.C. Stafford. Like most of his peers, Stafford commenced musical training at an early age, and before graduating from high school had composed a number of gospel songs and choruses for church choirs. He attended North Texas State University, Phillips University, and George Peabody College. Stafford put a great emphasis on the study of harmony and, as a result, published over 3,000 songs and authored three books of his choir choruses and one cantata, "The Kingdom of Love," plus a much-used textbook, *Harmony and Harmonical Activity*.

Stafford possessed a permanent teacher's certificate in the state of Texas, where he taught for many years. He held hundreds of singing schools in the United States and Canada, and was very active in assisting and aiding the maturation of gospel music and those people who labor in its behalf. He died in 1977, in an automobile accident, returning home from a singing.

Today, singing schools are still held in some rural areas, but for the most part, the youth prefer television, radio, record, and tape, if not live performance, and seem to wish to be spectator or performer, but not student. From the dawn of its birth until after the second World War, the gospel song depended almost entirely on the men who would travel the miles, teach the techniques and the songs, and maintain the oral tradition of teacher accompanied by songbooks.

Some few schools still exist; the Stamps School of Music is held each summer, and there are some others, but the era of publisher-composer-singer who took his songs and those of others to little schools in every hollow and valley is, sad to say, now gone.

It might be said that they are no longer needed, but somewhere the young people need to learn; that is assuming that the motivation for learning could somehow be kindled among them to burn with the intensity that propelled the pioneers of the first half of this century, determined and disdaining all else, to spread the melodies of Beulah Land.

Chapter 5
Tenors to Bass: The Gospel Singers

The church choir members and the convention soloists discovered larger audiences and a new sphere for their talents as the professional gospel singer emerged on the Southern scene. Unaware that they were pioneers, these men utilized the new medium of radio plus their public appearances to get their music out to the people.

Greenville, South Carolina, lies below the foothills of the Blue Ridge Mountains. A textile town, it is the home of Bob Jones University, the site of Shriners Hospital for Crippled Children, and a growing urban center for the palmetto and peanut counties which surround it. Lying in the heart of the Bible Belt and the gospel-singing South, this city has produced two names in gospel music which are intertwined with the growth and development of the field during and after the second World War.

Hovie Lister was born nine years later, but in the bitter January winter of 1916, Connor Brandon Hall began a sandlapper's life. Hall expressed an interest in and a talent for music at an early age. While still a boy, he "borrowed" his mother's guitar, and by trial and error taught himself to play. When his mother first realized her guitar was missing, she was rather angry and afraid that her son was just amusing himself and in his ignorance would harm the only musical instrument the family owned. But when she found Connor patiently picking and strumming and able to play chords from his favorite gospel songs, she was happy for his interest and encouraged his education musically in Greenville. Later he studied with Dr. John Hoffman in Atlanta and with other able teachers.

Beginning his career in 1932, he sang on a local radio station in Greenville. For the next few years he composed and taught singing schools, and as his career accelerated, he moved to Atlanta in 1942 to sing with the LeFevres.

Later, Hall organized the Homeland Harmony Quartet and sang tenor with this group until its disbandment in 1958. The Homeland Harmony had one of the first television shows in Atlanta and were on 55 stations daily. Hall's group made many recordings and personal appearances and was one of the most popular quartets in the years after the war. It was Hall who conceived the idea for the Homeland Harmony Distributors, which took gospel records to new locations and provided greater exposure.

By 1958 Hall's interests were moving in new directions, and upon dissolving his quartet, he became president of the Sing Recording Co. and worked in this capacity until 1960, when he became music editor for the Tennessee Music and Printing Co. In 1965 he became managing editor of the *Vaughan Family Visitor*.

Connor Hall has also worked as president of the National Singing Convention, and served for two years as a director of the Gospel Music Association. Encouraging and training young people in the field, he has been instrumental in the growth and expansion of gospel music, and remains prominent in the business today.

★ ★ ★

Villages surrounded the various cotton mills in Greenville, and from among these mill villages in 1926 came one of the all-time entrepreneurs and hustlers of gospel music. Hovie Lister began his piano lessons at a very early age, and paid for them by peddling Kool-Aid, ideas, and himself.

With an innate moxie and a determination born from the depression's insecurities, the 14-year-old Hovie persuaded his father and uncles, who comprised the Lister Brothers, to allow him to negotiate for them with the local station, WMRC. His effrontery won the family, with Hovie playing piano, a fifteen-minute program every Sunday.

Hovie Lister had confidence in himself and in his future, and his background of walking barefoot in the hot dust past the mill houses to the company store to purchase a 3-Center pop drink and a fried bologna and chili sandwich, gave him no pangs of inferiority. Life had been simple, but a jar of hellgrammites could catch a string of catfish and crappies which his mama rolled in corn meal and fried in a big iron pan on the wood stove on Saturday nights. And on Sunday morning before going to church, in attempts to fill out a skinny boy, there had been cathead biscuits, milk gravy, home-canned peaches, and sometimes, if the chicken yard was full, a young fryer cooked a delectable, crispy brown.

But all boys must grow up, and Hovie had left the ripe, bursting watermelons and the graveyard shift in the mill for the Stamps-Baxter School of Music, and eventually played for the Stamps-Baxter Lone Star Quartet. At seventeen he was invited by Connor Hall to play for the Homeland Harmony, which at that time boasted Jim McCoy, Otis McCoy, and "Big Jim" Waites. Then from 1946 to 1948, he worked as a gospel d. j. in Georgia and was at different times with the LeFevres and the Rangers.

October 1948 was the birth month for one of the biggest quartets in gospel music history. Hovie formed the Statesmen Quartet, the name borrowed from the newspaper of Georgia's Governor Talmadge. Mosie Lister, no relation to Hovie, was the first man to sing lead in the Statesmen, and, upon his departure, the part was taken by Jake Hess. Hovie, Hess, and Doy Ott were together about 23 years with "Big Chief" Wetherington joining them just a few years later. Jake Hess eventually left to create the Imperials, a successful and modern group, and later to organize the Jake Hess Sound which is heard today. When the Statesmen finally disbanded in the fall of 1974, Doy Ott, a member of the Oklahoma branch of the Cherokee nation, resumed his medical studies after a quarter of a century in gospel music.

During the fifties and sixties, the Statesmen were one of the most popular and most successful quartets on the road. For five years their television show, "Singing Time in Dixie," was aired over WSB in Atlanta. This program was different from many of the gospel music shows now seen, in that the quartet would do the show on location to prevent the flat look of four mikes and a backdrop. Many of the shows were filmed at a farm outside Atlanta, and some good-natured fun and horseplay went along with the singing.

Hovie Lister, the skinny little guy with the mustache, was intrepid before the challenges of new thought in his music, and at times the quartet was using harmony, arrangement, stage presentation, and techniques which were ahead of their time and which precipitated raised eyebrows and dubious looks. But the consensus of opinion must have been in their favor, because the Statesmen's innovations and trends were imitated by others. Altogether they cut 46 albums plus many singles, and sang the theme song for the film "A Man Called Peter."

A lifetime career friendship grew between Lister and the great James Blackwood, and with J. D. Sumner, who sang bass for Blackwood at that time. For many years, any program boasting the Blackwood Brothers was sure to have the Statesmen on the bill also. Personal friendship and business ventures went hand in hand as these three men worked to improve and expand the gospel music business. The trio was instrumental in forming the first National Quartet Convention and underwrote the expenses themselves for that first convention.

Lister has served as a member of the Board of Directors and as a vice president of the Gospel Music Association. Hovie Lister has been known as a musician and an aggressive agent in the gospel field, but he has also preached in church or concert when he felt it appropriate to do so. He was ordained in 1951 and served as the minister for the Mt. Zion Baptist Church in Marietta, Georgia, for 12 years.

During his career he has been dubbed an Arkansas Traveler, named as an honorary colonel in Oklahoma, Louisiana, and Georgia, and as an admiral in the Texas Navy. Burton College and Seminary in Colorado conferred in 1961 an honorary Doctor of Divinity Degree on Hovie Lister, and Georgia's Governor Talmadge called the Statesmen Quartet "Georgia's Ambassadors of Good Will."

Tenors to Bass: The Gospel Singers

The year 1978 finds Hovie Lister, at 51, a man still possessed of vitality and the same audacity that took the linthead kid from the cotton mill to national prominence in his chosen profession. It is the guess of his fans that he may be resting, but he is certainly not retired. Gospel music will hear more from this man yet.

* * *

J. D. Sumner, the tall, slow-talking guy with the big grin, has been billed over the years as "the world's lowest bass singer." His slouch is mimicked, his low-register notes imitated, and his kindness and generosity recognized by all who have met him face to face. Florida is his native state, as it was for promoter J. G. Whitfield, who became one of the top executives in the business, and owns *The Singing News*, a popular trade paper which annually gives the "Singing News Fan Awards" to favorites who the fans feel are the best in their category. Les Beasley, owner and manager of the Florida Boys and long effective in the advancement and workings of the GMA, is also from Florida.

After his discharge from military duty in 1945, Sumner joined the Sunny South Quartet, where he was associated with Jake Hess and composer Mosie Lister. In 1949 Sumner became one of the Sunshine Boys, and with Fred Daniels, now tenor and manager for the Blue Ridge Quartet, went with the group to California to experience a new phase of his career by starring with Charles Starrett and Smiley Burnette in several western movies.

The Sunshine Boys harmonized around the campfire and assisted Starrett in catching the bad guys; that is, after Fred Daniels learned to ride a horse the hard way—in front of the cameras with six-shooter in hand and villains in sight, but not the low tree limb that negated his vigilante spirit. But the Boys made recordings for Decca and Landworth Transcriptions and were probably one of the first gospel quartets to appear on network TV, and were the only group to have a network show daily.

Then in 1954, after a plane crash which took the lives of R. W. Blackwood and Bill Lyles, J. D. joined the Blackwood Quartet, and until his departure in 1965, was a favorite of the audiences. His popularity is evident in the classical live recording "On Stage—The Blackwood Brothers Quartet," made in Long Beach, California. The audience responded to J. D.'s bass and ready wit with overt enthusiasm. This was the first time that the true flavor and attitude of a gospel sing had been captured on record, and it is today a collector's item.

Through the years J. D. Sumner composed over 350 songs, including an album of Hawaiian music which holds a special place in the heart of its creator. However, his most popular song probably was, and is today, "The Old Country Church," still sung by the Blackwood Quartet.

J. D. Sumner was the originator of the idea of bus travel for gospel quartets, an idea which James Blackwood endorsed, Sumner perfected, and which has evolved into the luxury cruisers used today by performers in all fields of music. The National Quartet Convention was another concept born in the minds of J. D. and his close associates and nurtured and fostered into an annual event which grows appreciably in size and significance each year. The first convention was held in Memphis, Tennessee, in 1957 with J. D. Sumner, James Blackwood, and Hovie Lister picking up the tab.

In 1963 Sumner and James Blackwood purchased the Stamps Quartet Music Co., Inc., of Dallas, and Sumner has been manager and singer for the Stamps Quartet since 1965. He is also president of the Stamps Conservatory School of Music and the Gospel Music Co.

J. D. Sumner and the Stamps Quartet spent much of their time on tours, TV specials, and recording sessions with Elvis Presley. Presley, long a lover of gospel music, was incorporating more and more of it into his concerts, and featured Sumner and the group on "Elvis—Recorded Live On Stage in Memphis," as well as other records. But J. D. still keeps concert dates and close ties with the gospel circuit, and now, as always, it appears to be his life.

* * *

Otis L. McCoy was a trifle late Valentine present to his parents in 1897, born in a small town in South Carolina with the improbable name of Ninety Six. But the numerically named community wasn't far from Spartanburg and Greenville, and young Otis began at age 12 to study and to sing, traveling to such teachers as W. W. Combs, Glenn Kieffer Vaughan, and finally graduating from the Vaughan Conservatory.

Marrying and settling down in 1919, Otis followed in his father's footsteps and farmed the South Carolina fields of clay and sand, fighting the weevil, and picking the bolls. But a year later one of the tornadoes which so frequently ravaged and leveled homes on the flat, unprotected land, came twisting through to destroy his farm, and to cause him to reconsider his chosen lifestyle. Determining on a life in gospel music, he taught for 10 years at Lee College in Cleveland, Tennessee, and was editor for the Tennessee Music Co. for 23 years.

Working as a member of the Vaughan Radio Quartet, he sang for some years throughout most of the United States and in Canada. Then in 1936 he joined the Homeland Harmony Quartet, continued as a teacher in countless singing schools, and wrote over 200 songs. Today he lives in retirement and in the fond recollection of his many followers.

Leon H. Ellis, Tennessee-bred, moved to Florida in his youth during the depression years, and became a part of the gospel music movement in that state, which produced such names as J. D. Sumner and J. G. Whitfield. He attended several colleges and universities, and while at Lee College organized the Kingsman's Quartet. In 1950 he started the Happy Harmony Quartet and in 1960, in Baltimore, the Masters Quartet. He also worked as pianist for the Sunny South Quartet, and was affiliated with the Tennessee Music Co.

James Parks Waites, known as "Big Jim" or "Pappy," was the first bass singer to achieve national acclaim and was the grandaddy of all bass singers to come, with many attempting to copy his style and phrasing. He sang on radio, television, and records, and appeared at innumerable concerts through his rich life, which ended in late 1974. He was beloved by millions of gospel fans, and during the course of his career sang with the following groups: Morris-Henson Quartet, the John Daniel Quartet, the Electrical Workers Quartet, Vaughan

Radio Quartet, Stamps Quartet, the LeFevres, the Homeland Harmony, and the Rebels Quartet.

Bill Lyles was a bass singer who followed in Jim Waite's footsteps, and then became a favorite of the people on his own. Born in 1920 in Chattanooga, Tennessee, he attended the Stamps-Baxter School of Music. In 1947 he joined the Blackwood Brothers Quartet and was a member of the group when they won the Arthur Godfrey Talent Show in 1954. He was also a co-pilot for the Blackwood Brothers' plane, and later that same year, he and R. W. Blackwood were killed when the plane crashed. But Bill Lyles had possessed a unique bass voice, and he is still remembered for his melodious singing.

John Daniel worked for J. D. Vaughan and later for Stamps-Baxter. Then he organized the John Daniel Quartet, which sang over WSM's Grand Ole Opry, carried by NBC and broadcast nationally. John Daniel's quartet sang over WSM until his death, and recorded over the years for Columbia Records. During the course of his success, he employed 53 men in his quartet and was responsible for bringing to the public's attention such performers as Jim Waites, Jack Hess, Wally Fowler, Bill Lyles, and Tommy Fairchild. He introduced and helped make popular "Keep on the Firing Line," one of the songs reflective of the war years and obviously influenced by the jazz prominent in music in that day. The song was strong in counterpoint and was distasteful to those more accustomed to a predictable rhythm and not to a touch of the secular in their gospel songs, but the sound caught on and was relished particularly by the younger fans. John Daniel founded one of the first quartet publishing companies, and earned his place in the gospel sun not just for his discernible actions, but more especially for his influence, stimulation, and sway over those he met in the course of his life.

Nine years before the turn of the century, G. T. Speer, a man who was to found a dynasty in gospel music, was born in Georgia. Growing up in Alabama, he was reared in the heritage of religious folk singers and learned his fasolas along with his alphabet.

On February 27, 1920, Tom Speer married Lena Brock, sister of Dwight Brock, and with their children, the Speers spent their lives singing and propagating gospel music. To Tom and Lena were born Brock, Ben, Mary Tom, and Rosa Nell, each of whom in turn began to sing with "Mom" and "Dad" as soon as they were old enough to stand beside them in church or on the concert stage. Today, Mary Tom and Rosa Nell are proud grandmothers who have long since retired, but anyone familiar with the gospel field is aware that the Speer Family, led now by Brock and Ben, has won the Dove seven times for the Best Mixed Group in the business.

Brock Speer has commented that the lengthy extension of his bachelor days was simply because he was so completely involved in the singing career of his family that only in maturity did he begin a family of his own.

During his nearly 50 years in gospel music, Tom Speer worked first with the Athens Music Co., then he and Lena were employed by J. D. Vaughan and later by Stamps-Baxter. They were early pioneers of radio and TV, appearing on WSIX in Nashville and later on WLAC. In 1964, "Singing Time in Dixie," a syndicated television show, was filmed in Atlanta, and later they sang with the LeFevres on "Gospel Caravan."

"Dad" Speer taught hundreds of singing schools and composed about 600 songs, of which several are still often sung and much-loved, including "The Dearest Friend I Ever Had," "I Want to Be Ready," and "He is Mine and I am His."

He is Mine and I Am His

Now I know that He is mine and I am His forever,
He is leading me along life's way;
He'll be holding to my hand when I cross death's river,
He will take the sting of death away.

God's amazing grace sent down from heaven,
Rescued me from death and from shame;
Opened up my eyes and brought salvation,
Now I'm His, praise His holy name.

Now I know that He is mine and I'm His forever,
He is leading me along life's way;
He'll be holding to my hand when I cross death's river,
He will take the sting of death away.

Brock Speer was at one time chairman of the board for the Gospel Music Association and served for two years as its president; presently he sits on the GMA board and chairs the board for the Gospel Hall of Fame. As a producer for Skylite Records, he was responsible for what is said to be the first major gospel recording session in Nashville, using brass, strings, and a Nashville-arranged background. The result was the Oak Ridge Boys' record "Music City, USA." Considered by his peers and fans alike to be the impetus for the most professional group in the business, Brock Speer is a fine bass singer, an astute businessman, and an intelligent human being. He earned his Bachelor of Divinity degree at Vanderbilt University. With his pixie smile and his sincerity of purpose, Brock Speer keeps the interest and future of gospel music at the top of his priority list.

Able to sing as soon as he could talk, Ben Speer was playing the ukulele at four. He studied music extensively, playing a number of instruments, but specializing in the piano. Owner of the Ben Speer Music Co. and an expert in electronics, he operates what is probably one of the two best sets of sound equipment in the industry. He sets up and monitors the complex sound gear each year at the National Quartet Convention, and always meets and conquers the challenge that the dome-shaped convention center presents. Ben Speer is one of the most likeable people in gospel music; his warm personality and obvious good humor make him everyone's favorite, on and off the stage.

Chapter 6
The Paid Professionals

By the late thirties and early forties, quartets were known by name, and people quickly chose their favorites. The publishing companies were in fierce competition, and bitter rivalries were born which did not pale or die until the next generation came along, and sometimes not even then. Every congregation was visited, promoted, and hopefully persuaded to buy the songs and books of the company's representatives.

Behind-the-hand remarks about a competitor's talents were, sad to say, not uncommon. A favorite trick, sure to antagonize a performing quartet, was for an opposing group to time their entrance into the auditorium during the on-stage quartet's best number. The antagonists would create a commotion, shaking hands and greeting those present. Any milling around or loud talk or movement from those waiting their turn to perform, could always be counted upon to annoy and disturb the singers at work. But despite these rivalries, friendships were formed in those early days which were to endure for lifetimes.

The quartets formed by the publishing companies plus the independent groups were the beginning and first growth of professionalism in gospel music. Up to this point, only the songbook printers had made money from their music and were the only ones to have centered their livelihoods in its performance. Now in the early years of the twentieth century, the singers themselves packed their bags with gospel songs and pants with a fresh crease, and took to the road to sing for their supper and hopefully for the next day's meals too. The people of the shape note South were outraged. Peddling songbooks for a 10-cent commission had stretched the bounds of fundamentalist propriety to its breaking point already, but for gospel singers to expect payment for using their God-given talents was just too much. To charge admission for a gospel sing was unheard of, and, the people suspected, probably blasphemous.

Always a voluntary "love offering" had been collected by the resident minister and given to the visiting quartet. This was much the same way that the minister himself was paid; never any set amount, just what everyone could give. And if it wasn't enough to take care of the preacher's needs, then he just had to do without, as the people did when often they found distance between need and available means. The people thought this practice quite fair. Sometimes they would "pound" the preacher by bringing to the church sacks of meal and flour, jars of canned tomatoes and corn field beans, and sides or shoulders of cured pork. The quartets received a similar type of payment when invited to homes after the singings for country ham, grits, and red-eye gravy. And quite often a friendly soul would invite them to spend the night and awaken them the next morning with hot biscuits and freshly made molasses.

This hospitality was enjoyed and appreciated by the itinerant singers, but it didn't put the gas and oil in their cars that was necessary to keep traveling, nor did it support families back home. So performers became adamant and insisted on making a living; not necessarily a good one, but at least one adequate enough to provide gas and a tube of toothpaste.

The hard-shell Baptist moaned and groaned, and many a sermon was delivered against the gospel vagabonds with veiled threats of "cleansing the temple." There was opposition against the gate admission ticket even when the concerts were held in schoolhouses and town halls, and not in the churches themselves. The feeling was that men should not demand payment for singing God's music. But gradually the newness and strangeness of the concept of a professional gospel singer paled and faded. Slowly the people came to accept the company quartet man who got up at the convention and hawked his books, as well as the independent who stood to promote his group's next concert.

James Blackwood remembers a convention when, as he attempted to sell the Stamps songbooks, several insulted and belligerent listeners rose in anger to order him and his quartet from the church. The majority of the congregation, however, placed their sympathies with the Blackwood Brothers, and walked out behind the quartet to protest their dismissal. Many times the Blackwoods and other groups were booed by those who thought them merchants trafficking in the church's treasuries. The Southerners would often pay the small charge and attend a concert just so they could harass the performers with rude remarks and challenges to their veracity.

But the gospel singers themselves provided the solution to this problem. As the concerts were attended, for whatever reason, the people began to see the earnest sincerity and to hear the compelling testimonies of these performers. Looking at them with eyes now unclouded with resentment, they saw young men in their Sunday, if a little shabby, best—boys just like those down the road at the next farm: young, vibrant, enthusiastic, and always looking hungry. They had utilized talc and comb, knotted their bow ties with a flair, and sung their hearts out for any who would come and hear. Their love of the music and their optimism in its creed were infective, and the people soon succumbed to their smiles and to their songs.

If they could ride all night in a cramped-up sedan, wash the sleep out of their eyes at the pump behind the church, and then sing like heaven's own angels—well, how could you not welcome them? The hard shells began to crack, and the audience began to emerge, an audience which was to take the gospel quartet to its heart and sustain the romance to this day.

Thus far, only the gospel musicians who were born from a shape note heritage and raised in the influence and environment of a fundamentalist faith have been discussed. There were those who came late to gospel, but came to stay. Vaudeville thrived and prospered in the twenties and thirties, and from its concert circuit came performers who, seeing the popularity of gospel music in the South, began to incorporate some of this music into their programs. They, too, attended the singing conventions, to sing their newly learned gospel songs and to promote their next concert.

The influence of these vaudeville groups on gospel music was soon evident and reflected the country's musical tastes of the day. The afterbeat of the brass bands and the Sousa marches infected the music as well as glee club and barbershop techniques and tendencies. Henry Slaughter, five-time Dove winner for Best Instrumentalist, recalls his early days, when boogie-woogie was the rage, and its beat crept into gospel. According to Slaughter, most groups offered a varied program at the concerts. Doing the first half strictly with gospel numbers, they came back after the intermission for a second half of popular songs with catchy tunes and clever lyrics and with some plain old slapstick comedy which always left them in the aisles. They would close then with a gospel song, coming full circuit from where they had started. Working for the Stamps Quartet, Slaughter did his first piano solo at such a concert and played a fast boogie-woogie number.

This mixed programming continued until the late forties and early fifties, when the audiences decided that they wanted a specialized program, making it unprofitable to try to combine secular and gospel music. The theater groups had by now accumulated enough material to go full-time gospel and abandon vaudeville practices. Of course, these people made no pretensions of being anything other than entertainers, and the religious aspect of the music was seldom mentioned by them. Some of them, however, had assimilated the doctrines and beliefs expressed in the music, and embraced the gospel philosophy.

Chapter 7
Urias, Eva Mae, Alph: The Singing LeFevres

The year was 1921. William G. Harding was inaugurated President of the United States, and the women who had just voted for the first time watched their elected choice take his oath of office. In rolled-down stockings and hemmed-up dresses, the flapper was now a franchised voter. The historians say that this was the beginning of the "age of normalcy"; the people only knew that the shift from war to peacetime was a difficult adjustment. The cities were exploding with gang wars, bootleg liquor, and arrogant gangsters working all the angles. The United States, Great Britain, and Japan had their own arms race going as they built the largest navies ever assembled, and there were those who murmured and predicted danger. The affluent ones owned a wringer washer and a carpet sweeper, and the stock market gave no hint of what would happen in eight years.

In the mountains of Eastern Tennessee most families still used coal oil, T.V.A.'s electricity being still in the future. Money was scarce, but for the industrious, hams hung in the smokehouse and beans pickled in the crock. Plowing and tree snaking were done with mules or oxen, and the Victrola in the front room provided Saturday night's entertainment. Most of the churches were Baptist, and the baptismal font was as close as the nearest river. Vaughan songbooks came in by mail, and Sunday night would find the new shipment put to use by the eager singers. Some people would buy their own copies, and the family would gather with whatever musical instrument they had, be it Jew's harp or flat-top guitar, and practice the new songs.

Two brothers chose this time to walk out of the Tennessee hills and begin a journey which, more than 50 years later, is now completed. Urias and Alphus LeFevre were to become central figures in the heritage and history of gospel music. They remain major contributors even now, past their golden anniversary. The LeFevre brothers, sometimes accompanied by their sister Maude, began their career by singing in the churches found in the coves and glens of the Cumberland foothills.

Travel at first was on foot, and being good-looking young men and conscious of their appearance, they walked barefoot to preserve the polish and prolong the life of their shoes. Nearing their destination, they would stop at a creek or stream for an old-fashioned foot-washing, and then would arrive with a sparkling shoeshine and at times, a cut or stone bruise incurred along the way.

Both boys had early displayed musical talent, but perhaps Alph had been a little more anxious about his musical education. Having no money for lessons, Alph contented himself by standing under the window of the local music teacher and learning from his schoolmate's errors. Finally, the eight-year-old boy was discovered, and the teacher began that day the lessons which resulted in a fine violinist and an accomplished musician. The lady gave her time and talent to train and befriend a boy who has never forgotten her.

The boys grew into manhood singing at every opportunity and putting their earnings into their educations. Both attended Lee College, and Alph went on to Georgia Tech and North Carolina State Teacher's College.

Alph carried his violin and Urias his five-string banjo as the sassy little bay and the old buggy took them 15 to 20 miles a day. But there were churches over the next ridge and through the gap, farther than the little bay could manage, so they splurged and bought a Ford truck of the Chuck Wagon variety. To young men getting 5- and 10-cent admissions at their singings, this was quite an investment. Once they had collected the unheard of sum of 65 dollars and felt they would be financially fluid for at least a year.

Their travel now was mechanized, but the LeFevre boys were soon to discover that machines can bring problems of their own. The Chuck Wagon had magneto lights which meant that they worked only when the motor was turning very fast. In low gear, mandatory due to the deep-rutted roads, the lights simply didn't shine at all, so the brothers soon learned to take advantage of the daylight hours to travel, and to hunt a good camping place at dusk. Eventually they learned to cope with the vagaries of the old truck and felt confident enough to take their gospel songs and head West.

The Chuck Wagon took them to Oklahoma in 12 days of riding and 12 nights of hoot owls, fireflies, and beans and bacon. But the old rig's standard equipment did not include a heater or air conditioner. The midwestern sun boiled through the windshield and into the Wagon's engine. Frequent stops at passing wells were made to revive both man and vehicle. Lunch was canned sardines, hoop cheese, and saltine crackers bought at a local emporium and washed down with cold pop. The winds blowing across Nebraska and Kansas carried the grime that forecast the "dust bowl" soon to come. The dirt matted their eyelashes, invaded nose and mouth, and irritated and reddened their eyes. Grit coated them from head to toe, and their next bath was only as close as the nearest stream or river. The motels and rest areas of today's interstates were unknown then, and sometimes even the filling stations were many miles apart. But they made the trip safely and were emboldened by the warm Okie reception to their music to venture to new horizons.

And then it would rain. A hard downpour could transform a dry, dusty road into a long succession of mud holes in just a few minutes. What is now part of I-40 was then called the Broadway of America; however, only 16 miles of this "super highway" were paved. Needless to say, there were many stops when the old truck would mire to the hubcaps, and everyone piled out to gather limbs and sticks for prying and rocks for building a foundation. Once the boys found a brand new Ford coupe stuck in a roadside ditch. The owner sat sullenly in the car, and seeing an opportunity to lose his problem, he offered the Ford for sale at the ridiculously low price of 75 dollars. But he got no takers, because neither Urias nor Alph could figure a way to get it out either.

Anyone who has read William Faulkner's *The Reivers* will remember the story of the farmer who plowed up the road near his home, and then with the same pair of mules and for a handsome fee, would extricate the foundering automobiles. One suspects that the LeFevres met up with the same gentleman in the swampy outskirts of Memphis. At any rate, after becoming firmly entrenched in the quagmire, they agreed to pay 25 dollars to have their truck pulled by four horses through ten miles of muck. That hold-up amount was more than they sometimes made in a week, so they learned to avoid the Memphis marshes.

Once, in Cincinnati, Ohio, the weather forecasters predicted a cold wave that was rapidly moving into the area. Since the Chuck Wagon did not boast a heater, the boys quickly packed and headed her straight for home. But when night fell they were deep in Kentucky, and the temperature had dropped to ten below. They had put on all the extra socks, underwear, and clothes that they had with them, but this chill was unexpected and unseasonal, and their lightweight clothing was not adequate protection. Stopping by the side of the road, they made a quick pot of coffee and fried some salt pork for supper sandwiches. Afraid they would freeze to death if they remained still, they started out again, peering around the windshield in an attempt to see. No houses or lights were to be seen. Finally a building was discernible which proved to be a small jot-em-down store. The Wagon came to a stop, but when the men tried to get out, they found that their limbs were numb, their feet and legs almost frozen. Using both hands to pick up a leg and set it out, they were slowly climbing out when the storekeeper realized their predicament and with his wife rushed to help them. Taken into the store and set around the potbellied stove, the LeFevre boys gradually thawed out, thankful and happy, if a bit frostbitten.

The old Wagon finally gave up the ghost and was replaced by a Ford coupe which was driven until it reached its untimely end when its motor fell out right in the middle of the road. It was sold on the spot for 25 dollars, and the boys went car hunting again.

The young LeFevres were considered quite modern and progressive by their contemporaries. Since few churches had pianos, and even if they did they were certain to be out of tune, the brothers always carried their own instruments. The horrified and angry looks that drums and horns bring to the faces of the gospel conservatives today were equaled 50 years ago when the LeFevres walked in with banjo and violin. One man felt so threatened by the presence of the banjo in his church that he made a hasty exit through the window exclaiming that he "wouldn't stay in the church with that instrument of the devil."

The young men were also pioneers in the introduction of syncopation and progressive rhythm to gospel music. Singing at a convention in 1935, they were doing John Daniel's "Keep On the Firing Line," a very fast-paced and rhythmic number. Several listeners stood up and protested such jive music in a gospel sing, but immediately others jumped up and squelched their protestation—and the LeFevres kept on swinging.

There was little radio and no TV in those early days, so ingenuity had to be employed in their promotion work. Rolling into town in the early afternoon, they would quickly find a hall or suitable building to rent for the evening. Then Urias would drive up and down the streets while Alph, and whoever was traveling with them at the time, would stand out on the running boards and shout for all to hear that the LeFevres would be appearing that night at such and such a place. Combining this method with telephone calls made at random from the phone book proved a successful combination, and very frequently the hall would be so crowded that many people would have to stand outside and listen to the concert.

The most famous love story in gospel music began when the LeFevre brothers walked into a singing in a little rural Baptist church, and Urias saw the preacher's daughter enthusiastically playing the piano. Eva Mae Whittington was only eight years old, but her quiet beauty and long dark curls captured the heart of the sixteen-year-old Urias. Turning to Alph, he made the vow that this was the girl he was going to marry and he would simply wait for her to grow up. Eight years later he and Eva Mae were married by her father, and their lasting romance is in evidence today as they stroll hand in hand at the gospel sings.

Five children resulted from the LeFevre marriage: Pierce, Meurice, and Mylon work in various ways with their parents, and the daughters are Monteia and Andrea, who is now married to Jerry Goff and is a member of the Singing Goffs.

Eva Mae LeFevre sang alto as well as being proficient at the piano, and in 1933, with Urias and Alph, the LeFevre Trio was born. The tiny girl with the dark curls came to be called Little Eva Mae by the fans, and the second brother was known as Uncle Alph, his apparent warmth and good humor making him seem too familiar to remain a "mister."

Time passed and the radio stations began programming gospel music with some regularity. In 1940 in Atlanta, Georgia, the LeFevres began a daily radio show for the SunCrest Bottling Co. When asked what salary they desired, they considered and decided that they could be comfortable with 50 dollars a week. But when the first paycheck arrived, it became obvious that there had been a misunderstanding somewhere along the way. Each member of the group received 50 dollars individually! This was more money than they had ever seen before, and they were overwhelmed by the staggering amount.

They sang together through the years, with Eva Mae keeping alive their radio show in Atlanta and overseeing the production of their records during the men's absence in the war years. The fifties brought them to television with the "Gospel Caravan" and "America Sings."

In 1971 they celebrated their golden anniversary in gospel music. Fifty years of devotion to a career and to the people for whom they sang brought them reciprocal love and affection from their many followers.

During their years in the profession, the LeFevres have hired many people, making numerous friends and helping young performers. Rex Nelon of Asheville, North Carolina, has been with them, singing bass and working in the capacity of business manager, for over 20 years. In 1974, when Urias made the decision to retire and spend his next 65 years puttering around the kitchen and tramping through the Georgia woods for a little hunting, Rex took over the responsibility for managing the group. Uncle Alph and Eva Mae retired a few years later, and Rex Nelon has his own group today which attempts to keep up the LeFevre tradition.

The LeFevres are unique in the pages of gospel history. They were the first independent group to achieve full success and were one of the few professional gospel groups to stay on the road during the depression. They have experienced good times and bad; once they had to sell their furniture to stay on the road and keep singing until their fortunes rose again. Yet through it all, their faith has not wavered. Urias openly admits that if money had been his goal, he would have chosen another profession, since, as he says, "You can make a living in gospel music but you can never get rich." But they loved this music, they loved the people who came to hear them sing it, and they adhered to the basic precepts of its message. Their last hit record in 1974 with Urias still singing lead was "Stepping on the Clouds." The path of their lives has certainly been less than smooth, yet as they sang gospel's glad song, their hearts soared as did the hearts of their listeners, and for over 50 years their spirits "stepped on clouds."

Chapter 8
The King: James Blackwood

Alabama skies grew red from the flames of the crash. James Blackwood stood helpless as he watched the plane piloted by his nephew and his best friend drop to the earth and explode. It was 1954, and the Blackwood Brothers Quartet contained only two Blackwoods, R. W. and James. R. W. was only two years younger than his Uncle James. They had grown up like brothers and sang with their best friends, Bill Lyles the bass and Bill Shaw, tenor.

The quartet had gone to Clanton, Alabama, for the Peach Festival. The concert, held at the airport, was over, and preparations were being made to return home to Memphis. R. W. had taken lessons and had become a licensed pilot as soon as the quartet decided that the airplane was a definite improvement over a cramped sedan. The landing strip was short and night was approaching. There were no landing lights, and, as in previous situations, the singers had requested that the fans pull their cars to each side of the landing strip and flip on their headlights.

R. W. was concerned about the shortness of the strip, and the slight hump in its middle, so he proposed to make a practice take-off, just to get the feel of the small airport. At the last minute, a friend attending the concert, Johnny Ogburn, decided to go along with R. W. and Bill Lyles, who served as R. W.'s helpmate and makeshift co-pilot.

R. W. made one pass, nearly landed, but pulled up when he realized that his speed had overrun the short field. On his second pass, all seemed to be going well. R. W. touched down, then once again pulled up after some rough bouncing, but this time something went wrong. The plane suddenly nosed up in a vertical position, then turned downward in a screaming crash.

R. W. had been the son of James' older brother, Roy. Roy was born in 1900, James came 19 years later, and Lena and Doyle had appeared in the Blackwood household in the interim. Emmett and Carrie Blackwood had begun their family on a small farm in the Mississippi Delta, but had moved to Choctow County in 1923 to sharecrop.

Theirs was a religious family—regular church attendance, evening devotions—and all of them enthusiastic of the annual Brush Arbor Meetings which had replaced the camp meetings of an earlier day. In a wooded area, posts were placed in a horizontal fashion between tree limbs and were covered with brush to protect the revivalists from the elements as the days or weeks of the meetings took place. Rough wooden pews were nailed together, and the preaching and the singing lasted as long as the people could spare time away from their homes and crops. As did their grandparents before them, they came in wagons or on horseback, or even walked the miles if that was the only possible mode of transportation.

James Blackwood grew up in this atmosphere of Brush Arbor singing and basic fundamental religion. With his brother Doyle, he began singing the foot stomping songs when he was seven, and he never forgot those days that were for him some of the happiest in his life. The music and the message stuck; they spawned a career of over 40 years.

Doyle found an instrument unlikely in Mississippi soil, a Russian balalaika, which he taught himself to play, and he and James attended singing schools which stressed first the mesage of the lyrics, then perfection of the delivery of the melody and intonation. The boys were determined to become gospel singers, and James walked three miles twice a week to a neighbor's house just to hear the Vaughan Quartet on the radio. His own family couldn't afford such a luxury, nor did they have many of the necessities. However, it was a home of love, and there always existed a great closeness between the family members. When James was 12, Roy had his second son, Cecil, later to play an important part in the family singing.

After much study and determination, the first Blackwood Brothers Quartet was born in 1934 with Roy singing tenor, James lead, R. W. baritone, and Doyle bass. They walked the same route that all the gospel singers had to follow. Radio exposure came with WJDX in Jackson, Mississippi, and KWKH in Shreveport, Louisiana. Then V. O. Stamps stepped into their lives and replaced their broken-down jalopy with a new car, and got them bookings for more concerts for a percentage of their gross earnings.

They were singing from Stamps-Baxter songbooks such classics as "Just a Little Talk with Jesus" by Cleavant Derricks:

> I once was lost in sin but Jesus took me in,
> And then a little light from heaven filled my soul;
> It bathed my heart in love and wrote my name above,
> And just a little talk with Jesus made me whole.
>
> Chorus
>
> Now let us Have a little talk with Jesus
> let us tell Him all about our troubles
> He will Hear our faintest cry
> and He will answer by and by
> Now when you Feel a little pray'r wheel turning,
> and you know a little fire is burning,
> You will Find a little talk with Jesus makes it right.
> It makes it right.

The punctuation and capitalization of the chorus may appear a bit strange, but it must be remembered that this was quartet singing, and the whole group didn't sing all of the lyrics. In this particular song, the bass leads the way, and if written as it was sung it would look like this, with the short lines sung by the bass:

Now let us

    Have a little talk with Jesus

let us

    tell Him all about our troubles

He will

    Hear our faintest cry

and He will

    answer by and by

Now when you

    Feel a little pray'r wheel turning,

and you

    know a little fire is burning,

You will

    Find a little talk with Jesus makes it right.
    It makes it right.

In 1940 the Blackwoods moved their base to Shenandoah, Iowa, and sang over KMA, traveling to many states and gaining new fans and popularity. Then came the war years when they temporarily disbanded. R. W. was drafted, Doyle became ill and had to return home, while James and the others worked in an aircraft plant in San Diego. During these years, when they could get together and sing they brought gospel music to Californians who had never before heard its sound.

After the war, the quartet moved back to Shenandoah, and Bill Lyles joined them as the bass singer. Roy and Doyle retired permanently from the concert stage to handle the group's record promotion and mail order division. With Roy gone, Bill Shaw became the new tenor.

The Blackwoods' final move was to Memphis, Tennessee, in 1950, and in 1951 they began recording for RCA, the first gospel group to do so. In 1954 they won the Arthur Godfrey Talent Show and achieved national prominence. James, R. W., Bill Lyles, and Bill Shaw made America aware that gospel singers were on the scene to stay.

However, 1954 was the fateful year, and the deaths of R. W. and Bill Lyles brought James Blackwood to a grief unknown to him before, but also to a faith now tested and found to be stronger for the test. When James sings "I'll Meet You in the Morning," he sings of loved ones, eventually including his parents, whom he knows that he will see again.

There was a temptation to give up, but James felt that his message was one that needed to be carried, so R. W.'s younger brother, Cecil, stepped in as baritone, and a lifetime friendship began when J. D. Sumner began singing bass with the Blackwood Brothers Quartet.

By 1955, the group traveled in a bus, a first for the business, and in 1956, they once again won the Arthur Godfrey Talent Show. The year 1956 was also the occasion of the first National Quartet Convention, which the Blackwoods and the Statesmen Quartet had underwritten and endorsed. It was held in Memphis, although later the site was changed to Nashville. Skylite Recording

Company came into existence with the assistance of the two quartets who felt a need for an all-gospel recording company of outstanding quality. For a number of years the two quartets had performed together on a regular basis. Deep friendships grew between the members. Hovie Lister and the Statesmen were, for many years to come, sure to be on the bill if the Blackwoods were singing. They combined business and friendship, and the friendship continues among the men.

A song each quartet loved to sing, and the people enjoyed, was the popular "Sweet By and By":

> There's a land that is fairer than day,
> And by faith we can see it afar;
> For the Father waits over the way,
> To prepare us a dwelling place there.
>
> In the sweet by and by,
> We shall meet on that beautiful shore,
> In the sweet by and by,
> We shall meet on that beautiful shore.

—Arrangement by Clyde Williams

The harmony is much more complicated than the simple lyrics depict: it was the ability of these men to take a few words and create a complete production number which would stimulate the audiences to cry for more.

In 1961 the quartet bought the Stamps Quartet and Music Company. A few years later J. D. left the Blackwoods to personally manage and sing with the group. The birth of the GMA in 1964 was another dream of James Blackwood which had become a reality.

Now, in 1978, Cecil and Jimmy, son of James, are the only Blackwood members of the quartet. James, due to failing health, appears only after the quartet has completed the major portion of the program, then comes on stage to sing three songs, the last of which is always "I'll Meet You in the Morning."

The trimming of his concert time is a concession to his doctor's advice, but to James Blackwood it is a great personal loss. He once announced upon arriving on stage, "I've been waiting all night to get out here." As his quartet sings, he stands in the wings, clapping and encouraging them. Obviously anxious to join them, he sincerely believes the gospel creed, and he has the charisma to impart his love and faith to others.

Once a newcomer to gospel music was eagerly standing backstage, anxious for a first glimpse of the man about whom so much had been heard, so much written, so much said, that it was difficult to guess what might be fact or fiction. The evening wore on, and still Blackwood did not appear. The newcomer became impatient and turned to a friend, an oldtimer of gospel sings, asking how to recognize James once he did come. The friend just smiled and replied that when a man came in who looked as if he were a king, then that would be he.

The anxious one was a little incredulous, perhaps not experienced in gospel music, but sophisticated enough to have met politicians, dignitaries, and great men of letters, and he felt doubt that one singer could carry an aura of the purple.

After a bit more impatient waiting, the newcomer glanced up at the stage door and in strode—not walked, but strode—a man whose bearing showed that he paid homage to none, and who wore his regality without condescension.

The novice was awed and realized that this man really fit the image that people had generally projected. He was not very tall, but carried his body with grace, his head slightly thrown back. His hands were fragile, but had an obvious firmness which dispelled any suspicions of weakness. As he moved, the lights struck the leonine head and were reflected by the fair hair. He was not striking in any particular feature except perhaps the nose, which was a trifle long. His was the image cast in bronze masks and sculptured from clay to preserve Greek philosophers, Roman statesmen, or princes of the realm. The one remarkable characteristic of the face was that it proved to be unforgettable; it was James, and perhaps that is the highest compliment that a man's mirror might pay.

The doubter was impressed, but still not convinced. He lingered at the concert, waiting and listening as James sang and talked, touched the people and felt their response; and the truth began to emerge. The nobility of this man was real, but it came from within himself, a genuine outpouring which by its own strength had developed into obvious physical manifestations. The man's face reflected his own soul. It was not a conscious effort on his part, but came as the result of his total immersion in his faith and in his complete dedication to its demands and its imperatives. It would appear that mind, body, and soul had all been fused into a being with a singleness of purpose. The total unity and complete absorption of James Blackwood sets him apart; he is his faith, he is his music.

Two of the songs which James often sings, and which capture his philosophy, are "Ten Thousand Years" and "Now I Have Everything."

Now I Have Everything

I had nothing but heartaches and trouble,
I was seeking for fortune and fame;
I had nothing but doubts and confusion
But now I have everything.

Everything I need to make me happy
I have Jesus to show me the way!
He has saved me
And He gave me life eternal!
And now I have everything.

—*Charlie Yandell and David Ingles*

James Blackwood is like a photograph which has not been touched up to hide blemishes or imperfections. However, sorrow, anger, and frustration are not alien in his life. He is not as quick to temper or as given to impatience as perhaps are some others, but he also has his limit, that point beyond which he cannot be pushed. Secure within himself, he has the confidence to rely on those with whom he works. Supportive of innovations and willing to give any suggestion his consideration, he has integrated all which was of worth into making his quartet one of the leading groups in gospel music for more than 40 years.

Once a reporter for a local television guide, with a circulation of only a few thousand, went to him with an article which had been published and which dealt largely with his work. The reporter gave Blackwood the article and requested an interview for yet another column to be printed in the little magazine. Blackwood suggested that the writer meet him in about 30 minutes, then seating himself behind the record rack at his table, proceeded to slowly and meticulously read the article, no comma or conjunction escaping his attention. Finally, after giving the material his full concentration, he walked over to the waiting reporter, asked that he be seated, and gave an hour and a half of his time to fully answer questions and to add unsolicited but useful information. His concern did not lie in the number of people this article would reach, but rather that he could enunciate that which is so important and vital to him, and he has always taken his opportunities where he found them, from nationwide TV to the church with a membership of 200.

James Blackwood has no sense of being someone extraordinary, and certainly never envisions himself as a "star." His assurance and confidence have grown from the swaddling clothes of love and early religious affiliation, to the certain confidence in his maturity that he stands on solid rock. To himself, he is now and has always been a gospel singer with a message to carry. But chopping cotton taught him pragmatism and practicality, for gospel singers have to eat and pay the bills if they are to continue their careers. Consequently, he feels it not in the least demeaning to stand before the audience after each concert and announce the records which his quartet offers for sale. It is just a part of his profession, which is part and parcel of him. The Silver Eagle with its intakes of diesel fuel is just another means, as was the magazine column, of reaching out to the people.

The joy which permeates and is radiated from his body has grown from the seeds of his creed, and its vitality and virility emit from his soul and encompass the man. James Blackwood has fulfilled what he felt was the mission of his life, giving of himself and his talent until his mission and himself are one. He makes all who hear wish to be with him in that morning:

> I'll meet you in the morning, with a "How do you do"
> And we'll sit down by the river and with rapture auld acquaintance renew.
> You'll know me in the morning, by the smiles that I wear,
> When I meet you in the morning, in the city that is built four square.

Chapter 9
A People's Music

The depression of the 1930s dealt cruel blows equally to the South and to the North. Soup lines formed on Chicago's Dearborn Avenue and on Atlanta's Peachtree Street. The employed became the itinerant, and the derelict the man of the day. Hunger hovered over the tenements of the big cities and threatened the sharecroppers' shacks on the Delta. Men could no longer trust their government, their banks, or their employees; each in turn had failed them.

In the South, the families of folk song heritage felt the keen blade of deprivation, but had one last resource to which they could turn. The faith of their fathers sustained them once more. In a joyless world of starvation, drought, and near hopelessness, their God and His optimistic music brought them comfort, hope, and a joy of contentment in the faith that He would not forsake them. Fortified by bowls of potato soup, the men and women in the Appalachian Mountains and the goober counties of South Carolina would gather at their churches for prayer and solace, believing in a better world to come most certainly, but right now, even more importantly, they believed that this world offered more than the tears of today, and that these troubles and heartaches could be overcome with an enduring faith.

The strength of these people lay in their determination to live, for rather than passively accept the perils that befell them, or look only for relief in another time, another world, they firmly believed that their God could fortify them and enable them to withstand whatever the present brought them, and that if tomorrow was no better, than perhaps the day after would be.

Realistic and pragmatic, they understood the natural order of things. They knew that in turn the old must pass away to afford breath and space for the young to survive. And they looked toward death not simply as a release from this life, but as the normal progression in the evolution of all life. Pain was expected, for it was part of birth and was never considered a punishment for sins committed, but as the natural result of experience in the human cycle. Searching no rationalizations for the bad times, they accepted them as they did the tares with the wheat, not apathetically, but simply with the recognition that they did exist.

So they anticipated the day when the sun would again shine, they worked and walked through each day with the sure and certain knowledge that it would eventually come, and they gritted their teeth and bided their time. And when the clouds finally lifted, and the pressure was eased from their shoulders, the smiles were quick to come and the dormant happiness and excitement in simply being alive to see the day, spilled into their voices and their laughter. They had survived, they had overcome; with their omnipresent God and their unswerving tenacious faith in His love for them, they had once again beat the famine stalkers, the sickle-bearing desperations of this world. The panic of hopelessness had never pulled them down, and they stood on the top of the mountain to greet the sun of the new day.

Most certainly the mothers of the depressed South needed a stalwart and unbending creed. Winter winds blew against the newspaper stuffed in the old house's cracks, and formed ice in the water bucket sitting on the kitchen table. Fuel was scarce and often stolen. The children huddled in bed and felt the Fahrenheit bitterness. The larder was barren save for some corn meal and dried beans. If there were some salt pork left to cook with the beans and some potatoes left in the cellar, then these women felt indeed fortunate. When the winters grew more fierce and the provisions dwindled, hunger would hollow the children's eyes and the mothers would look away and go into the empty fields and orchards to grub for frozen apples or sweet potatoes once overlooked.

The men fished the rivers and hunted the ridges and hollows. Possum, groundhog, and mud turtle were heartily welcomed to the cook-stove, and the early creesy greens of spring brought tears of relief. Christmas was celebrated primarily in the church, for there was no money for necessities, let alone gifts. Warm clothes were cherished, and the crocheted shawls of another day were unraveled to become mittens and caps.

The rural schools were closed on the most bitter days, too cold for the boys and girls to walk the distance in blanket coats and shoes worn thin. The teacher watched her class crowd the wood stove and lunch on a boiled potato, and saved her pennies for Christmas candy and maybe a bag of oranges.

Many died, mostly the very young and the very old, and they were buried to the tune of "Amazing Grace" and with "influenza" on their death certificates. But the mothers' eyes did not blink and close, for there were the living still to care for. Fifty cents could be earned by scrubbing down a washboard someone's laundry. The coins were hoarded for precious commodities, flour and salt. When the diseases of childhood were complicated by the ill-fed bodies of the stricken and the cold in which they lay, the local physician came to comfort and sometimes heal for the price of a cup of hot coffee and a promise of payment on a better day.

The women cooked with molasses as their sweetening and the precious salt their only spice. The livestock were kept alive at almost any cost, for when the mule or oxen died, the land could only be plowed by the physical endurance and stamina of the man's sweat. The women followed the plow to drop and cover the seed, and thus began the season of muscle-rending labor necessary to grow and harvest the crop. Shoulders became bent and heads drooped beneath the burden and struggle of trying to stay alive. In their eyes the smoldering fire of their faith still glimmered, as they stooped in the dirt to pull the weeds and to curse the drought that threatened to defeat them, but at the same time to praise the God they knew had not forsaken them.

Under the summer sun as it was under the winter's chill, the land was quiet. The roads saw few travelers, and the gospel caravans of music teachers of old were almost gone. Few braved the fury of July's heat or January's cold to teach and to peddle their gospel songs. Things were now uncertain, and the once-full pots of squirrel and dumplings or rich beef stews were now barren of their riches and hung empty on the hook. The hearty adventurer who now pressed his bony steed from farm to village had to accept the corn meal mush and thin blanket of the times.

Some few persisted and, riding on hope and a worn saddle, shared the people's fate, eating the slim rations blessed by the prayers of those not yet defeated. If the church could boast no firewood, the itinerant teacher would gather the faithful in a proffered kitchen, and if little was learned, all were heartened and cheered for just having sung the gospel songs. On hot sultry nights, the people would return to the ways of another day and meet on a meadow's hill or town's green. The music revived them, and for a little while they could forget the perils of this year's crop and also last year's hunger. But if no teacher came, the older ones helped the younger, and the old songbooks were literally sung to shreds.

The people did not laugh; the sounds of merriment had disappeared. The creak of the plow and the smack of the loom broke the silence which had gone undisturbed since the Sunday hymns had pierced the quiet. The air hung heavy and pressed against the chests of the silent men and women; it reeked of poverty's privations and choked the weak and the doubters. Quietly they walked through the 1930s, a few teachers of songs and their own ministers their only companions, save for their God. But the optimism never left their music and they never gave up hope. When the era of hardship ended, they looked around and found that the rest of the country had survived too, and they knew it was because they had faith in their Maker if not in anything else. If man had survived, then he surely must have put his reliance in Someone stronger than himself, or so they thought.

The people of the South had articulated their faith in their music as they had done since they had turned from Psalm-singing to soul-singing. The core of strength which had held them together during the depression had been discernible and vocalized only in their hymns of praise and prayers for endurance. The nights of fearful vigil spent by the bed of a baby racked with whooping cough had been passed by the wide-eyed mother as she softly sang the words of a comforting hymn and rocked to and fro. And if her vigil had been in vain, then her comfort came in the promise sung about a new morning and a meeting day.

The songs written in these years of trial reflect the needs and hopes of the people living each moment only too vividly.

Beyond The Sunset

Beyond the sunset,
O glad reunion,
With our dear loved ones who've gone before;
In that fair homeland we'll know no parting,
Beyond the sunset forevermore!

—*Virgil and Blanche Brock*

Jesus Took My Burden

Yes, Jesus took my burden
I could no longer bear,
Yes, Jesus took my burden
In answer to my prayer;
My anxious fears subsided,
My spirit was made strong,
For Jesus took my burden,
And left me with a song.

—*Bertha Mae Lillenas*

The cotton was picked and the tobacco was cut as the laborer hummed a gospel tune. The people answered the admonition to "Have a little talk with Jesus,/Tell Him all about our troubles." The day's work was always accompanied by a song, and the song carried the wave of optimism. The normal questions of a man would be answered by and by as "Farther along we'll know more about it,/Farther along we'll understand why." If sometimes a man doubts or has his fears, then he turns to his source of strength: "Oh, Jesus is a Rock in a weary land,/A shelter in the time of storm."

Although few people could afford to buy the songbooks, they were still being written. The few composers who dared to walk poverty's paths and take music to the people were remembered as beloved teachers. Dad Speer conducted singing schools and received farm produce in lieu of cash to help pay for his travels. At the church not so fortunate as to host a singing teacher, visitors from adjacent counties who had heard some of the new songs would teach their brothers and sisters the new melodies of faith. The oral tradition born nearly 200 years before still supplied the music, and the people congregated regularly to sing their cares away. The LeFevres are said to have been one of the few professional gospel groups still on the road in the thirties. Traveling with a confidence that never left them, they criss-crossed the Bible Belt, bringing a welcome song to any who would hear. Fried fatback and milk-sop gravy on biscuits fortified their bodies, and a lasting belief sustained their souls. The singers or teachers, the handful who came to cheer and comfort, to share and solace, have never been forgotten by those who felt their caring interest.

★ ★ ★

The land had been silent under the depression, but the guns of war burst that silence with a shattering blast, and some of the pieces were never to be found again. Jobs were available for the asking, and a man could easily earn enough to feed his family now; but if he was young and strong, he was snatched from the family circle and given a helmet and a rifle. One fear replaced another as mother and father, wife and sister watched him walk away on dusty roads that had once led to hunting trails or a neighbor's home. Hunger had been the common foe; now the men left to fight in places unheard of and unknown, and even the enemy was mostly a vague threat. For after the years of the fight for survival, politics and geography were foreign elements and the Germans and the Japanese merely specters about whom the politicians spoke. Those left behind clung to each other for comfort and support, and could not understand why a man spared winter's pneumonia and exhaustion's collapse, must go to fall under an alien's gun. Male and female roles were reversed as the women worked the mule or succumbed to a mill's doffer to provide the family's bread. There might be more money now, but there was little available to buy. Deprivation came not from an inability to buy, but from an inability to find the goods. Molasses once more replaced the sugar in the morning coffee, and finally it was considered fortunate if the coffee could be had.

The victory gardens were simply another way to attempt to feed an army and the homefront at the same time. Canneries grew from the necessity of preserving the harvests, and beans, peaches, and mustard greens were sealed in glass jars. Meat was again scarce, so squirrel and rabbit wound up on the pantry shelf next to the blackberry jelly and chow-chow made fiery with cayenne pepper. The children learned their geography by the battle sites and knew Normandy and Belgium better than Utah or St. Paul. And they learned a different lesson taught by the subtleties of American propaganda: hate was permissable, even encouraged, if directed toward anyone of Aryan descent or with sloping eyes.

The patriotic ballyhoo was not to be denied, and caught up in its frenzy were those who were still shaking their heads and trying to comprehend this newest calamity. There was much talk of God and country. No public meeting or gathering began until prayer had been offered for the safety of our fighting men. Even the schools where opening exercises had not been stressed before, now started each school day with devotions of prayer and Bible reading, followed by the Pledge of Allegiance and singing of the National Anthem. The mothers and wives had stars to hang in their windows, each a badge of pride for the men in service. They longed for letters from the man so far away and hovered along the path from house to mailbox. But all feared the telegram and prayed for deliverance from its finality.

The roads were now crowded with buses and trucks bearing smooth-skinned boys looking out with fearful eyes and dreading the ship's journey to a probable death. At home they were not yet considered men, and this responsibility lay heavily on a child's shoulders. In desperate clutches at life and an attempt at posterity, they married childhood sweethearts or girls they had just met while at bootcamp. As often as not, the seed they had sown was born a fatherless child. In their frantic rush toward death, they left behind a girl who, experiencing at once war and birth, became a woman.

For the parents waiting at home, the monthly allotment checks were one small blessing. The winters came with deep drifting snows and sleet which iced the trees into glassy apparitions of beauty. But now there was money for kerosene to fill the lamps and cut into the winter's darkness. Christmas was a gayer time now if the boys were home on furlough; if not, then black walnuts and sugar that had been hoarded back went into cupcakes and were sent abroad with a knitted muffler, a letter, and a prayer.

The churches were more affluent than in the previous decade, and after the program of solemn white-sheeted angels and little boys dressed in their bathrobes and foil-covered crowns, Santa came to give each child a bag of Christmas candy, nuts, and oranges. On Christmas Day a laying hen that had ceased to produce was stuffed, and with a little imagination looked just like the turkey in Norman Rockwell's dinner on the cover of *The Saturday Evening Post.* There could be presents now, and a rosy-cheeked doll, or a ball glove that smelled funny and new and wonderful all at the same time, might be found under the tree. In the city, carolers strolled the streets, and in the country gathered at the churches, to light candles and sing "Joy to the World." The lonely, the afraid, the widowed, and the hopeful came to petition mercy and deliverance and to request a comforting Presence.

> Just a closer walk with Thee;
> Grant it Jesus, if You please,
> Daily walking close with Thee,
> Let it be, dear Lord, let it be.

This song typifies the anxiety and the loneliness of those who walked and watched and waited the long days of the war. The people cried out for reassurance, for something sane in a world crazy with bloodshed. They believed in God, they had not doubted Him, they just had a very real need to feel that He was indeed with them, that He was close by their side.

Now I Belong to Jesus

> Jesus my Lord will love me forever,
> From Him no power of evil can sever...
> Now I belong to Jesus, Jesus belongs to me,
> Not for the years of time alone, but for eternity.

—Norman J. Clayton

Like poor frightened children, they clutched at their God and wanted His love reaffirmed and His presence with them reassured. Their songs said that if God was with them, then they could withstand "what 'ere betides," and so they sought a closer relationship with Him whom they trusted.

Be Thou Near

> When my heart is filled with sorrow, Be Thou near;
> When I fear to face the morrow, Be Thou near.
> Be thou near me, O my Saviour,
> When my heart is filled with fear;
> When I feel my faith is failing,
> Blessed Saviour, Be Thou near.

—Oswald J. Smith & B. D. Ackley

A new familiarity sprang from this urge for close communication. Rather than a fearful Diety of thunderbolts and judgment, God was viewed as a friend, a close companion. The seeds of this familiarity grew for 30 years and produced "Jesus Christ: Superstar" and the Jesus movement. But in the forties, each fighting man wanted to take God to war with him, and each seemed to claim His personal concern and interest. "God is my co-pilot," they said, and they carried pocket testaments to prove it.

Dearer Than All

Jesus entreats you in Him to confide,
Make Him your constant companion and guide;
He can do more than the whole world beside;
Jesus is dearer than all...
No friend like Jesus my soul can enthrall,
Jesus is dearer, far dearer than all.

—Alfred H. Ackley

Their compelling exigency assuaged, the people were reassured and emboldened, and walked out to meet the contingencies of the day and to sing hymns of thanksgiving.

The Love of God

Oh, love of God, how rich and pure!
How measureless and strong!
It shall forevermore endure
The saints and angels' song.

—F. M. Lehman
Arrangement by Claudia Lehman Mays

Heavenly Sunshine

Heavenly sunshine, heavenly sunshine,
Flooding my soul with glory divine;
Heavenly sunshine, heavenly sunshine,
Hallelujah! Jesus is mine!

—Arrangement by Charles E. Fuller

★ ★ ★

Step right up and see the show,
Sinners there, in the front row.

Hellfire and brimstone, there is no doubt,
Await those who are holding out.

The women cry and the children fear,
Don't worry, the evangelist is near.
Heal the blind, the halt, the lame;
Do it all in God's own name.

Hell hath no fury like a canvas-top preacher,
And down they come, out of the bleacher.
To confess and be saved is a good thing to do,
But what about tomorrow, when there is just you?

The treaty was signed aboard the battleship *Missouri*, and the people made the sharp cybernetic turn from war to peace. The age of technocracy had already taken its first fledgling steps, and now it raced through the twentieth century. Highways became super-highways, then interstates with myriad ramps and exits. As fast as the builders could throw together grease racks and pine-scented restrooms, the big oil companies lined these new turnpikes with their stations. Gasoline flowed freely from the pumps, and Goodyear and Goodrich continued their struggle for number one, as once-rationed products became plentiful for all. When the concrete bands criss-crossed America, the traveling evangelists picked up their tents and hit the road.

Oral Roberts brushed the Oklahoma dust from his gabardines and informed the world that he was God's own instrument of healing grace. A seven-year-old boy stood on a chair to tell of his visions and recite the sermons that he had learned phonetically. Bob Jones University graduated intense young men who walked the main streets of Southern towns and on hot summer Saturdays, would pause for a few minutes under the awning at Woolworth, wiping their faces with freshly ironed handkerchiefs. And to many kids growing up then, there came to be a very real connection between frayed shirt collars, the soul's salvation, and the smell of hot popcorn coming from the dime store. These young men were sincere in their ministry, and they would not have believed the simple truth, that their exhortations turned more people away from the church than into it. The apostolic urge was given free vent, as these men chose their topics and their territory, and unleashed their oratory on the street corners.

Sinclair Lewis didn't invent Elmer Gantry. Con men and charlatans have been around since the first honest minister passed the plate and gave them the idea. And as was their insidious intent, they mingled with the true shepherds until it became almost impossible to distinguish wolf from herder. They trampled the insecure, demanded money, and frightened and confused the American people as from different corners was heard the voice that claimed the solitary route to salvation.

A retired Lutheran minister propagated his "magnificent obsession" with the publication of *The Robe* and *The Big Fisherman.* Lloyd C. Douglas created a panoramic view of those near Christ in such epic dimensions that it was no wonder that Hollywood snatched them up for their lavish productions of loincloth romance and near-religious piety. The message seemed to support a soul-shaking experience, an undefined Diety, and the command "to go and sin no more." From the questionable taste of a God of cinerama and stereo sound, American heads turned to Norman Vincent Peale and his *Power of Positive Thinking*. The philosophy of optimism and teeth-gritting and jaw-squaring "I can do it," was embraced by some, questioned by others, and rejected by those who found it impotent against the Berlin Wall or the cobalt bomb.

Billy Graham took the eyes of Ezekiel, a cultured Southern accent, and an apparent sincerity of purpose into the pulpit, and began the crusades that have touched the lives of more people than were affected in the old wars between Christendom and the infidels. To the people, his words rang true, and for a large number, he became the foremost religious authority in this country.

The major denominations grew, prospered, and evangelized, and the Christian religion, in varied forms and aspects, appealed to the people, many sincerely adhering to its tenets. Itinerant Bible-thumpers and honest clergy alike urged a personal salvation, a dedicated life, and a re-affirmation of faith. And traveling different routes, the people followed their consciences into a modern, progressive world. Still straining to discern sheep from goat, they put their trust in a God well known to them; even if some of His ministers fell short of the mark, He did not.

However, gospel music fans don't seem to be as easily duped as those whose trust sometimes gets between them and their better judgment. Any performer or promoter will quickly tell you that the first things an audience looks for when a group walks on stage are sincerity and honesty. No matter how intense the testimony or how enthusiastic the singing, the antennae of the listeners seem to catch the mendacity of the ones on stage. People raised on a gospel diet appear to be capable of sensing the true attitudes, and if the vibes don't feel right to them, they just sit politely and listen, but they don't come back.

On November 8, 1948, Wally Fowler held the first all-night singing in Ryman Auditorium in Nashville, Tennessee. Fowler was the actuator and instigator of a new format in gospel music. Up to this time, gospel was sung in concerts by only one, or sometimes two groups. Of course, the conventions were still being held, and were well-attended, the gospel singers making the convention circuit regularly. A few groups had begun hiring promoters who, before the group's arrival, would rent a suitable building and advertise the forthcoming performance.

An all-night singing was something comparatively new, a different approach which the people immediately endorsed and supported. Four, five, or even six quartets would be hired by the promoter, usually for a flat salary. He would then buy radio spots and newspaper ads and distribute handbills, anything he could afford or imagine to bring in the crowds. With well-known groups and for a nominal admission, he could usually fill the house. The quartets would each perform for about 20 to 30 minutes, and a 7:30 p.m. sing ended at one or two in the morning. So the audience had received five or more hours of entertainment for the original admission price.

* * *

The contrived never has the power or the impressiveness of the natural and the real. The true emotion, the unforgettable experience, result from the harmonious blend of a mutual concern and desire. The parade of gospel performers across the stage at an all-night singing offers a wide spectrum of abilities, forms of presentation, and personal philosophies. Each in turn strives to please with pop-rock sounds, old-fashioned revival songs aimed to stir the emotions and arouse the senses, or with smooth professional performance and well-produced numbers.

The audiences tolerate some, admire others, and flat out love those with whom they can best identify and who, more than the rest, verbalize their own hopes and dreams. But for the most part, they enjoy it all, and when at intermission they ply the vendors for cokes and chili-covered franks, they speak of their favorites and fail to comment only on those who appeared to have greased their hands from the oil of the anointed without having first made the covenant for its possession.

The same groups re-appear for the second round, this time giving an abbreviated program, and then it is the last. The singers most popular, most beloved, have the closing minutes with the people. It is about one o'clock in the morning and the hall grows quiet. A little weary, the audience is yet anxious and expectant, for this is what they have been waiting for, this is what they came for. Previous songs and fine performances were enjoyed, but they were just the preliminary for what is about to happen.

These people are here because they want to be here, but beyond that, because they wanted the opportunity to participate in a communion of kindred spirits. It is not a congregation of diverse denominations and dogmas, nor is it a congress of diverse opinions and divergent viewpoints. The God they serve and the theology they embrace are peculiar to all and alien to none. The songs now are of a riper age, and several times the people are asked to join in the singing. On stage, the group begins the old familiars which have been much requested, and as the words strike into the recesses and collide with the working vibrations in the depths of all who hear, an almost involuntary response rises from those depths and searches for expression.

The song goes on, and in answer to its pledge and its promise, one by one, hands are raised, stretching upward, wrists arched back, palms open and flat as vessels which await a filling and a function. The open hand is a commitment, a re-affirmation of a vow made in joy and remembered in pleasure. The singers come down to touch the people, and in the clasp and embrace, the experience of an unquestioned hope and a satisfying resolve unites them.

It is unique—a large assembly agreeing on purpose and destination. The dissensions of lesser issues do not trespass here, and the freedom born from being among those of similiar persuasion makes permissable the independent word or gesture. Neither the tear nor the smile are deemed out of place, and if a man wishes to grasp the arm of his son and bless one much loved, then all witness and share his happiness and may be prompted to express an emotion shadowed before by an innate timidity.

Chapter 10
Black Gospel Music

From the hopeless song of the first black slave who sailed up the James River in 1619 to the joyous singing of Andrae Crouch on a concert stage in 1978, the history of black religious music does a complete reversal from utter desperation to praise and thanksgiving.

Andrae Crouch was the first Negro to cross the color lines in gospel music. His compositions are sung by all the major groups in white gospel, and his personal appearances brought the first integrated audiences in the music's history.

Crouch's music ranges from rock to melodic songs. Playing the piano as he sings, he is backed by his group, the Disciples, and whether the beat is hard or soft, the response is great to this performer of gospel music who broke the invisible color boundary. There is little similarity between the ecstatic songs of Crouch and the songs sung by slaves for over 350 years. "My Tribute" is one of Andrae Crouch's most widely known songs:

> How can I say thanks for the things You have done for me?
> Things so undeserved, yet You give to prove Your love for me.
> The voices of a million angels could not express my gratitude;
> All that I am and ever hope to be—I owe it all to Thee.
>
> To God be the glory, to God be the glory,
> To God be the glory for the things He has done.
> With His blood He has saved me,
> With His pow'r He has raised me,
> To God be the glory for the things He has done.
>
> Just let me live my life—let it be pleasing, Lord to Thee;
> And should I gain any praise, let it go to Calvary.
> With His blood He has saved me,
> With His pow'r He has raised me,
> To God be the glory for the things He has done.

★ ★ ★

The heritage of black gospel music can be clearly traced back to the dense forests and jungles of Africa and the lush tropical Caribbean Islands. A people enslaved, freed, and then oppressed have produced, over the years, music which has reflected their desperation and fear as well as their determination to overcome persecution.

The African people sang and danced with a rhythm and syncopation peculiar to their culture; this singular talent had no counterpart on earth. They sang for many reasons: religious celebrations, burials, and social occasions created the need for appropriate music. In the middle and upper regions of the Niger River lived the Mandingo and Malinke tribes, who had official singers, Jillikes, which performed at the chief's request, often merely to flatter and placate their ruler. At other times these "court singers" would be summoned to perform before visiting dignitaries, telling in song of the greatness of their tribe and some of its individual members. As in all cultures without a written language, an oral tradition was necessary to preserve historical events.

Thomas Bowditch, in 1817, wrote *Mission From Cape Castle to Ashantee*, relating the habit of the Africans there of using music to tell stories. One story he relates concerns the people's belief that a type of preying mantis, indigenous to that area, had the magical power to kill animals simply by looking at them with their large and protruding eyes. The African story-song describes how a sheep or goat would stumble upon the mantis, become transfixed by its eyes, and after swaying violently to and fro, would finally fall over and die. Some songs of these people were allegorical, others dealt with love and everyday life.

The natives of the dark continent, as well as the various islanders, were accomplished musicians on many types of instruments. Drums were very popular and were made in varying and unusual shapes. Stringed instruments, cymbals, and horns were all employed by different groups of these black people. A vast store of musical knowledge came with the captives sent to America in bondage.

Hard Trials

De fox hab hole in de groun',
An' de bird hab nest in de air,
An' eb'ryt'ing hab a hiding place;
But we, poor sinner, hab none.
Now aint dat hard trials, great tribulation.
Aint dat hard trials, I'm boun' to leabe dis world.

Many slave women would sing lullabies to their children in their native tongue; the children would remember these songs and pass them down to their offspring, until generations later, when all knowledge of what the words had meant was gone, the feeling of a soul enslaved and in torment remained, and the slaves continued to sing the old songs in sorrow.

Arriving in a strange land with a strange language, the blacks attempted to learn the new speech, but the harsh sound of the letters, G, D, and R were very difficult for them. These sounds they just excluded from their speech altogether, or else they slurred over the correct enunciation. Many of the English words they misunderstood and consequently misused. In the Negro spirituals, accepted as the classic black music, the meaning of many of the words is not known because at the the time of their first singing the people were incorrectly pronouncing words, and now their definition is obscure.

The Negro spiritual has been known by several terms. Generically they are known as "shouts," plantation songs, mellows—the Negro word for melody—or sorrow songs. But whatever name is used, the spirituals were the original folk songs of the black, and today they are considered to be the true music of the Afro-American.

Slaves sang for many reasons. Sometimes it was their own choice, in other instances it was a command. A silent slave wasn't a good slave. The masters had various reasons for wanting the blacks to sing. On the plantations the overseer could tell where the slaves were as long as they were chanting, and also he could follow the progression of their work in the fields as the voices grew farther and farther down the rows. The sick humor of the overseer standing over a black with whip in hand saying, "Sing, you happy nigger," is not an exaggeration. The master and the overseers would prod the silent slaves with "make a noise" or "bear a hand." In the North, the canning companies in Baltimore and other cities instructed their slaves to sing, as did the Mississippi River dock captains. The wharves were noisy with the Negro work songs as they loaded and unloaded the cargo vessels. A slave's ability to sing was considered a part of his worth, and if the black could play a musical instrument, then he was fairly sure of good treatment.

During the long summer evenings, the slaves would be called from their quarters to the plantation house to sing for "massa" and his family and guests. Each estate had at least one slave who could play the fiddle or banjo, or "banjar," as the Negroes called it. The American banjo was similar to a stringed instrument found in certain African villages, and the slave probably made his own from memory in a free life, and passed that knowledge down to others. The white owners enjoyed the rhythm and tonal quality of their chattel's music, but they would have been quite upset if they had caught on to the double meanings many of the Negro songs held. While the blacks sang of "going to Canaan's land," they were referring to an earthly freedom as well as a spiritual one.

In the South, Christmas was a big celebration for the slave. It was the one day that was a true holiday, and while once again they sang for their owners, it was still Jubilee Day and gifts of fat back, shoes, and even sugar came their way. There was no work, and on most plantations each male slave was given a small allotment of spirits, usually rum. The North, with its industrial lifestyle, did not often make Christmas a special day for their Negroes. Slaves were purely a business investment, and there was never the "darky" concept, the good old nigger who had worked long and hard for his kindly "massa."

At first, church-going was not considered proper for the blacks. They were not thought to possess souls; consequently there was no need for any attempt at salvation. However, in time, the owners felt that perhaps they had been wrong, maybe the slaves should become proper Christians. It was assumed that the blacks were probably practicing voodoo or some heathen rites, so an exposure to Christianity was deemed in order.

At first the slaves went to the white churches. Balconies away from the whites were their designated seating spaces. The master and his family rode to church in their carriage, and either the overseer or a trusted slave followed behind with the blacks in a wagon.

However, the services of the white people were not to the liking of a breed who were more accustomed to spontaneity and vigor in their religious celebrations. The blacks were quick to accept the white God, and saw in the person of Jesus a personal Savior. As Christ had been a Messiah to His followers, the slaves saw a Deliverer who would someday remove the chains of their bondage and set them free. They identified quickly with the lamentations of the wandering Jews, their captivity in Babylon, and their final release to their homeland. The spirituals they sang often referred to the Hebrews, and parallels were drawn between the plight of the ancient tribe of Israel and the slaves' own sorrows. When they sang of freedom for the captive Jew, they were thinking of themselves, although they never let the whites know that they held such treasonous thoughts.

Babylon's Fallin'

Pure city, Babylon's fallin', to rise no more,
Pure city, Babylon's fallin', to rise no more.

Chorus

Oh, Babylon's fallin', fallin', fallin',
Babylon's fallin' to rise no more.

Oh, Jesus tell you once before,
Babylon's fallin' to rise no more;
To go in peace an' sin no more;
Babylon's fallin' to rise no more.

If you get dere before I do,
Babylon's fallin' to rise no more;
Tell all my friends I'm comin' too;
Babylon's fallin' to rise no more.

Frederick Douglass at 21 was an escaped slave whose friends raised the money to buy his freedom. He became a lecturer for the Anti-Slavery Society and traveled in the North and Europe. He was the establisher of the newspaper *North Star* and wrote three autobiographies. His grandson was Joseph Douglass, who was the first Negro concert violinist to tour the nation. In *Readings in Black American Music,* edited by Eileen Southern, there is a passage from the autobiography of Frederick Douglass. Experiencing the terrors of slavery himself, he wrote of the blacks and their music: "The songs of the slave represent the sorrows, rather than the joys, of his heart; and he is relieved by them, only as an aching heart is relieved by its tears. Such is the constitution of the human mind, that when pressed to extremes it often avails itself of the most opposite methods. . . . Sorrow and desolation have their songs, as well as joy and peace. Slaves sing more to MAKE themselves happy, than to express their happiness."

Since their church-going was as structured as their work in the fields, the slaves yearned for a freedom of religious expression. Some slaves became preachers, feeling the need to speak to their fellow companions in captivity. Secret meetings were held in the forests and marshes of the South as the slaves stole away from their cabins in the middle of the night to listen to one of their own tell them of their Savior Jesus and His ability to free not only their souls but their bodies as well. Silently, they slipped through the darkness, stepping on soft patches of turkey paw and fallen leaves. Gathered in a close circle, their brown faces glimmered in the soft light of the single pine torch. In hushed tones they sang their traditional folk hymns whose melodies had been brought from Port Royal, St. Helena, and West Africa. Familiar spirituals such as "Nobody Knows De Trouble I've Seen" were sung on the Sea Islands so long ago that their origin is unknown. The slaves changed the lyrics to this and all their songs through the years, mainly because the performance of each tune was spontaneous and whatever words seemed fit at the moment were sung. It was many years before these folk hymns were put to paper, keeping a continuity of lyrics.

Some of the expressions so often found in the spirituals came from sources in the past, and there are several explanations for these phrases. The chariot found in "Swing Low, Sweet Chariot" and in many other songs is believed to have gained its significance from a legend born in Rhodesia. In *Negro Musicians and Their Music* by Maud Cuney-Hare, this particular story is found. It seems that the natives who lived near Victoria Falls gave their dead chief a unique funeral by placing his body along with the paraphernalia of his rank and food for his journey into a large canoe. The canoe was then freed to float toward the Falls. The people would stand on the shore and sing as their deceased leader floated toward the brink. However, the story relates that once, as the chief neared the Falls, a chariot was seen to descend from the mists; the chief arose from his canoe and the chariot took him heavenward.

Another expression imbedded in many of the spirituals is of "de valley" or "de lonesome valley." Many sources report that this phrase simply refers to this lonely valley of life, such as is found in Psalm 23: "though I walk through the valley of the shadow of death." Another more colorful suggestion is reported by Thomas W. Higginson in his book, *Army Life in a Black Regiment*. Higginson served as colonel of the first slave regiment, the South Carolina Volunteers, became an active abolitionist in the Underground Railway, and was fascinated by the songs of his black soldiers. *Readings in Black American Music* gives his version of the "valley" symbolism. It seems that before a young girl was to be baptized, she tied a handkerchief around her head with a peculiar knot. From that moment until the time of her baptism, perhaps some days later, she would not change the clothes she was wearing so that her cleansing in the water would be complete. A girl going through this period before her river baptism was said by the slaves to be in "de lonesome valley."

Eventually the whites did not feel endangered by the thought of slaves having their own churches and services. Perhaps the delicate noses of some of the white ladies sitting beneath slaves who had little opportunity for personal hygiene helped motivate the men into giving the blacks religious freedom. The black services differed greatly from the more sedate worship of the whites.

After the people were assembled, the first person to feel spiritually moved would stand up and begin a song. Others joined in and all present clapped vigorously. There was always much foot-patting and clapping, so musical instruments were not necessary, although cymbals, piano, and guitars appeared in some churches. Moaning filtered through the singing, and the sound continued until mutual consent and the need for rest caused them to return to their seats. The preacher would read a passage from the Bible, then the impromptu chanting would begin again. Some individuals testified as to their personal experiences and happiness, while the congregation rose a few at a time and began a rhythmic swaying which eventually became stronger, and bodies would be writhing as mouths spoke in unknown tongues. Extemporaneous shouts were joined by improvised songs until once again they quieted and the minister stepped to the pulpit.

The fiery sermon spoke of sin and salvation, hell and heaven. The unsophisticated oratory prompted more singing and dancing. Anyone physically capable of doing so joined in, even the small children awakened by the near-hysterical shouting. After the collection was taken, "repentance chairs" were placed in the front of the church, and any who felt that the moment of redemption was upon him sat as the elders gathered around and prayed in loud and strident voices for the acceptance of this soul into the circle of saints. The singing had never ceased; it rose and swelled with the joy of seeing a relative or friend sitting in the seat of the redeemed. These celebrations lasted as long as four or five hours, and all left physically exhausted, but spiritually uplifted.

In some churches a more formal meeting was held, but after the quiet of the decorous rites, the congregation joined in a circle, shuffling, singing in an energetic burst of religious fervor. This spontaneous and instinctive dance brought criticism from some whites who felt that it was a throw-back to an African heathen ritual.

Similar to the paths taken in white gospel music, the blacks instituted singing schools and discovered the excitement of camp meetings. In 1791, Newport Gardner opened the first black singing school in Newport, Rhode Island. There were fewer schools for the Negro, but the ones that did exist were well attended.

The open air, natural settings of the camp meetings were to the liking of a people accustomed to rejoicing under the stars. However, the slaves were made to sit behind the preachers' stand. While at many meetings rough benches had been made for the whites, the blacks had Mother Earth for their seats. The lack of physical comfort was common to them, and they did not object to looking at the preachers' backs, but they felt regret at not being allowed to join in the invitation given at the meeting's end. Whatever soul might have felt the prodding to go forward and find salvation's touch had to remain in the back and express the new-found emotion with his own group. Often the blacks would move away from the meeting place, and holding handkerchiefs, would form a ring and dance, an action which they thought necessary for their spiritual anointing. However, the masters assumed that it was a voodoo dance of some kind and had no place in a Christian setting. The more educated blacks deemed these dances a disgusting recall to a primitive past which they wished to forget. But the "Praying and Singing Bands" were a pledge of faith for many slaves, and without the dance they were afraid that entrance into heaven was not absolute.

In 1787, a number of slaves left Old St. George's Methodist Episcopal Church in Philadelphia. They formed the African Free Society, from which two churches evolved, St. Thomas African Episcopal, and Bethel African Methodist Episcopal with Richard Allen as pastor. Branches from the Society established churches in various cities, and in 1816 the first independent Negro religious denomination in the United States was formed. The A. M. E. Church held its first general conference and elected Richard Allen bishop.

Allen compiled hymns just for his congregation, and in 1801 published the first hymn books by a black for the blacks. *A Collection of Hymns and Spirituals from Various Authors, by Richard Allen, Minister of the African Methodist Episcopal Church* and *A Collection of Spiritual Songs and Hymns Selected from Various Authors by Richard Allen, African Minister* contained a large number of hymns by Isaac Watts, a couple by Charles Wesley, and many old spirituals. There were 64 in one book and 54 in the other. Many of the hymns composed by white men were changed by the blacks, who added lines and phrases, and incorporated them into spiritual use. A number of blacks considered the use of white hymns and the changing of the old spirituals to be a serious threat to their musical heritage.

In 1841 and 1842, the first choral singing in a black church was heard. Many church members became upset and left their home church, feeling that music was for the entire congregation; choirs and anthems were not part of the black's history. There arose an argument over instruments being allowed in the services. Congregations were split in their decisions. In the A. M. E. Church in Baltimore in 1848-1849, musical instruments were permitted for the first time in that denomination's short history. Several churches utilized their choirs by holding concerts and raising money for the needs of the church.

The Negroes sang few secular songs, and most of those were working songs. Chanties were sung on clipper ships and on steamboats from the Ohio River to the Rio Grande. The word was sometimes spelled chanty or else shanty. The latter version was thought to have come from the black's shanties along the river's banks. In some instances, the slaves were used as rowers, and the practice of singing while rowing came from Africa where, as on any oar-powered vessel, a cadence was necessary to keep the proper rhythm.

Another form of work song was the "corn" or "shucking" music. Gathered from several plantations, the slaves would shuck the harvest of corn and sing to relieve the monotony of the job. This was not sweet corn for the dinner table, rather it was hard corn used as feed for the farm animals as were the shucks which were made into silage. Also some of the hard corn was ground into meal for bread, grated into grits, or soaked in lye to make hominy, whole kernels of corn later cooked with butter and a common dish on all plantation tables. Other secular songs were lullabies, children's songs sung at play, action songs, and rounds.

Also there was the music of the street vendors. Strolling the streets with baskets of crabs or fresh strawberries held balanced on their heads, Negro women sang of their wares. George Gershwin caught the color and atmosphere of the street vendor with the strawberry woman of Charleston in *Porgy and Bess.* Other blacks carried cured moss for kindling and posts which could be used to prop clothes lines. The origin of the most famous of the black work songs, "John Henry," is thought to have come from the story of a Negro who died in the building of the Big Bend Tunnel in West Virginia.

Few love songs were known to the slaves and few were sung, because the very real possibility always existed that the loved one could be sold and sent away. The slaves practiced the ceremony of "jumping the broom" and later even had church weddings, but it was always with the knowledge that tomorrow could bring a forced separation. Some of the secular songs reflected the slaves' quest for freedom and the knowledge that there were always the patrollers, poor whites who hunted slaves for pay, waiting in the darkness for any black who attempted to escape.

Run Nigger, Run, De Patteroler'll Ketch Yer

Run, nigger, run, de patteroler'll ketch yer,
Hit yer thirty-nine and sware 'e didn't tech yer,
(Repeat several times)

Poor white out in de night
Huntin' fer niggers wid all deir might,
Dey don' always ketch their game
D'wat we fool um is er shame.

Run, nigger....

My ole mistis promus me
When she died she'd set me free,
Now ole lady's ded an gone,
Lef dis nigger er shellin' corn.

Run, nigger....

I seed a patteroler hin'er tree
Tryin' to ketch po' little me,
I ups wid my foots an'er way I run,
Dar by spilin dat Gentleman's fun.

Run, nigger....

A song now and then was just for fun.

Juba

Master had a yaller man
Talles' nigger in de land,
Juba was dat feller's name
De way he strutted was a shame.
Juba, Juba....

Oh, twas Juba dis and Juba dat
Juba killed de yeller cat
To make his wife a Sunday hat.
Juba.

Minstrelsy originated on the slave plantations. With little entertainment available, the whites looked to the blacks for amusement. On warm evenings the Negroes were called to the porch of the big house, where the master sat with his family to watch the show provided by talented slaves. Instrumentation was banjo and bones. Sheep or goat ribs were blanched white and were struck together in a powerful rhythm to accompany the dancing of the blacks. Simple comedy was provided as the slaves capered about in slapstick antics. The whites enjoyed the impromptu dancing and comic acting. These mandatory shows gave rise to the myth of the "happy nigger."

Professionals in black face appeared on stage before 1830. A quarter of a century later, when the blacks themselves began putting on minstrel shows, they found that they had to copy the white interpretation of Negro singing and mannerisms in order to be accepted. However, the music and the performance increased in quality as the blacks created their own shows. "Lew Johnson's Plantation Minstrel Company" along with George B. Hicks' all-Negro "Georgia Minstrels" in 1865 achieved a great deal of popularity with black and white audiences. However, from 1875 to 1895, the minstrel shows decreased in tasteful performances; the music became gaudy and commercial. The fantasy of a happy, shuffling creature who was lazy and carefree had become the accepted image of the Negro. To escape this demeaning caricature, the blacks turned to classical music. But the minstrel shows had been the forerunner of the musical comedies and vaudeville in which both the blacks and whites participated.

Stephen Foster crossed the color line in the 1840s and 1850s with his songs of "Old Black Joe" and "Swanee River." He rode the crest of the wave of the minstrel popularity as shows came to every big city. The North had heard little of the black people's music, and the plantation songs were a novelty to the Yankees.

After the Civil War, white missionaries went South and greatly influenced the now-freed slaves. Unfortunately, their musical impression on the songs of the blacks was a negative factor. The African strain of their heritage and the wild impulsive style gradually changed in many instances to a bland mixture of black spiritual and white gospel. The two did not mix, and the result was a colorless and insipid music. Many of the Negro churches quit singing the old spirituals altogether. The freedmen now wished to imitate the genteel worship of the whites and began to sing only white hymns. The Negroes had never sung in parts. Improvisation by the entire congregation had been their style, and harmony was unknown to them and alien to their musical history.

In New Orleans in the mid-1800s, a section of the city was known as Congo Square. There the blacks gathered to sing and dance. The call and response pattern was a frequently used style, and the music from the Caribbean Islands combined with the French-Creole patois to produce a stirring sound. "When the Saints Go Marching In" was a funeral song. After the deceased had received a proper burial, the mourners were accompanied home by a band which played joyous music to console the mourners, and also because the Negroes felt that the dead were dead, and the living should turn from sorrow and seek happiness. The brass bands played this popular song and others with the jazz sound which was growing steadily in popularity. Many cities claim its birthplace, but New Orleans is generally considered to be the cradle of jazz and the blues.

Jazz and blues were the music of the blacks. The whites were very quick to recognize its merit and beauty and began trying to reproduce the sound, but the greats of jazz were black. W. C. Handy composed "St. Louis Blues," the old-time classic. The list of composers and performers of this music reads like a Who's Who of jazz and blues and also ragtime: Will Marion Cook, Duke Ellington, Count Basie, Cab Calloway, Lionel Hampton, Fats Waller, Louis Armstrong. The list could go on and on. The influence of the jazz sound was soon heard in the gospel songs which the Negroes were singing, and the jazz, blues, and ragtime style is still found in gospel music, black style.

The blacks created their own musical comedies. Then they turned to classical music. By the beginning of the twentieth century, the first black ballet was performed, and the first black opera was heard. The first black classical composition is believed to have originated as early as 1840. Famous works in classical Negro music include: "Kykunkor" ("The Witch Woman"), a dance opera by Asadata Dafora Horton; "Le Niagara" and "L' Americaine," composed by Lucien Lambert, who studied in Paris; "Negro Folk Symphony" by William Dawson; and "Afro-American Symphony" by William Grant Still. At any rate, musicians and composers came upon the American scene with such talent and greatness that the cultured whites and even the press had to give them recognition. Harry T. Burleigh, composer, singer, and writer, was a black man of fame and genius. The Spingarn Achievement Award, established in 1914 by J. E. Spingarn, chairman of the executive committee of the NAACP, is given each year to a man or woman of African descent who has made the highest achievement in any field of human endeavor. In 1917, Harry T. Burleigh was given the Spingarn medal for excellence in the field of creative music, and in 1929 he received the Harmon Foundation Award and 400 dollars for his arrangement of Negro spirituals and instrumental suites. In 1925, Roland Hayes received the Spingarn Award for "the reputation which he has gained as a singer...and because in all his singing Mr. Hayes has so finely interpreted the beauty and charm of the Negro folk song."

In *The Negro and His Music*, Alain Locke provides a chart which categorizes the periods of black music between 1830 and 1936: The Age of Plantation Shout and Breakdown, before 1830; The Age of Sorrow Songs, 1830—1850; The First Age of Minstrelsy, 1850—1875; The Second Age of Minstrelsy, 1875—1895; The Age of Ragtime, 1895—1918; The Jazz Age, 1918—1926; The Age of Classical Music, 1926—1936.

Since the book was published in 1936, Alain Locke was not able to complete his chart, but since the depression there have been the freedom songs of the civil rights movement, classical compositions, popular songs reflective of the day, and gospel music. Roland Hayes, the black tenor who made America sit up and take notice of a black Caruso, was followed by the beautiful operatic voice of Marion Anderson. William Grant Still, Thomas Anderson, Hale Smith, and Carman Moore are black names which must be mentioned in the field of classical music, for those men composed and created music for all America.

One of the major schools founded at the end of the Civil War to educate the free black was Fisk University in Nashville, Tennessee. George L. White formed a choir, the Fisk Jubilee Singers, which became the most famous black group in the nation. The singers preferred to perform classical music, but the audience response told them that the spirituals were what the people wanted to hear. The Jubilee Singers were the first black choir to sing before kings and queens of Europe. The choir members wanted to forget the slave days, but the people wished to hear "Didn't My Lord Deliver Daniel?"

In 1874, Thomas P. Fenner published *Religious Folk Songs of the Negro*. Fenner was the director of the original Hampton Student Singers of Hampton Institute in Hampton, Virginia. This was another college established to teach the freed blacks, and it is still in existence. Thomas Fenner's Student Singers traveled across the country and in Europe singing both classical and spiritual music.

In 1892, the Bohemian composer, Anton Dvorak, wrote "New World Symphony." He had come to this country to direct the New York Conservatory of Music. After hearing the Negro spirituals, he composed his symphony. "Swing Low, Sweet Chariot" appears in the second theme in the first movement. Many white Americans were surprised at the inclusion of black music into a classical work, but Dvorak had heard some of his students singing the old folk songs and was charmed by their beauty.

W. E. B. DuBois, 1868-1963, attended Fisk University, received his Ph.D. from Harvard, and continued his studies in Berlin. The Massachusetts black researched Negro history and wrote a collection of essays, *The Souls of Black Folk*, published in Chicago in 1903. DuBois was a militant and joined with others of his philosophy to form the Niagara Movement in 1905. The group was composed of young militant intellectuals. In 1909, the Movement joined with both blacks and whites of the same political persuasion to become the National Association for the Advancement of Colored People. In *The Souls of Black Folk*, DuBois wrote one essay on the music of his people. The following is a short excerpt from that essay: "They that walked in darkness sang songs in the olden days—Sorrow Songs—for they were weary at heart. . . . They are the music of an unhappy people, of the children of disappointment, they tell of death and suffering and unvoiced longing toward a truer world, of misty wanderings and hidden ways."

The civil rights movement in the early sixties brought its own music. Born in the churches, the songs of freedom were sung by demonstrators as they marched, as they protested with the sit-ins, and as they sat in the jail, arrested for their attempt at equality. In *Readings in Black American Music*, Mahalia Jackson discusses the importance of the freedom songs during the fight for the black's complete emancipation. She quotes a minister as saying, "The singing has drawn them together. Through the songs they have expressed years of suppressed hopes, suffering, and even joy and love." A comment from Martin Luther King, Jr.: "The Freedom Songs are giving people new courage, a radiant hope in the future in our most trying hours. . . ."

According to Miss Jackson, the songs began to be sung during the Montgomery boycott. The students made up new words to fit the spirituals and gospel songs they had been singing. Some of these new songs were recorded, others were passed among the people in the old oral tradition. At times when the protestors were jailed by the hundreds, they would sing to keep up their courage and the white jailors would join in the singing. Just before Christmas of 1962 in Albany, Georgia, Dr. King led a march to protest denial of the right to vote. King and the marchers were arrested. Upon release, King, along with Ralph

Abernathy, was arrested for praying on the steps of the City Hall in Albany. Each time, and there were many times, the Negroes were jailed, they sang. Singing to gain strength and withstand oppression was long the black's mode of defense. The slaves had sung "We Are Climbing Jacob's Ladder" and "Oh, Freedom," a spiritual derived from an old hymn, "The Heavenly March." "We Shall Overcome" was the theme song of the movement, but it was written especially for the current crisis. "Oh, Freedom" was a Sorrow Song that fitted the occasion.

Oh, Freedom

Oh, Freedom! oh, freedom! oh, freedom over me!
An' befo' I'd be a slave, I'll be buried in my grave,
An' go home to my Lord an' be free.

Oh, freedom! oh, freedom! oh, freedom over me!
An' befo' I'd be a slave, I'll be buried in my grave,
An' go home to my Lord an' be free.

No more weepin' over me,
An' befo' I'd be a slave, I'll be buried in my grave,
An' go home to my Lord an' be free.

There'll be singin' over me,
An' befo' I'd be a slave, I'll be buried in my grave,
An' go home to my Lord an' be free.

Thomas A. Dorsey is recognized by many as the first composer and performer in black gospel music to achieve national acclaim. Dorsey was born son of a country Baptist preacher about 1902. His father was paid, as were many of the white ministers, in good food and farm produce, but his was a musical family and he was able to study with a teacher in Atlanta. Later he attended Atlanta Baptist College. Dorsey began his musical career as a blues singer, but in 1923 began singing gospel music. Dorsey had used jazz, movement, and syncopation in his piano blues, and he carried this style over into gospel music. As had happened in white gospel, many of the black ministers objected to the foot-stomping, shouting type of religious music, even though their ancestors had worshipped in such a musical setting. Yet, while some of the Negro churches clung to the old songs which were white in derivation, or toned down to a more "respectable" sound, many accepted the new gospel style which was really more African than American.

"Precious Lord, Take My Hand" and "Peace in the Valley" were Dorsey's two biggest hits, although he also wrote "Someday, Somewhere" (his first song), "Sometimes My Burden is So Hard to Bear," and "Come Unto Me All Ye That Labor and Are Heavy Laden and I'll Give You Rest."

The National Convention of Gospel Choirs and Choruses, Inc., was the black equivalent to the GMA, although it never managed to organize and achieve a solid national success. Its headquarters is located in a building constructed during the early 1970s. The modern, air-conditioned structure replaces an old building which served as both a school and a home for gospel singers. Thomas Dorsey has served as president of the National Convention, and as assistant pastor of the Pilgrim Baptist Church in Chicago. Dorsey's closest companion on the gospel stage was Sally Martin, who sang with him for years and is now the national organizer for the Convention.

Gospel music is different from the old spirituals in that the blacks did not sing in parts, but sang as a group with occasional shouts and outbursts not totally related to the song being sung. However, through the years, with the choirs of Fisk University and Hampton Institute and others like them, the Negroes began to harmonize. In gospel music their new talent of part and solo singing came to the fore.

Mahalia Jackson was born in New Orleans in 1911. Raised a Baptist, but influenced by the lively music of the Holiness Church, she, like Dorsey, put gusto and power into her interpretation of gospel songs. Many of the jazz musicians moved from New Orleans to Chicago, and Mahalia went with them. During the depression she sang with Robert Johnson and the group was known as the Johnson Gospel Singers. Chicago is probably the birthplace of black gospel music; although it was sung in other parts of the country, the professionals, for the most part, got their start in the windy city.

Analogous to the white gospel progression, the black singers began performing for nickels and dimes. Mahalia Jackson traveled with Thomas Dorsey for a time, and sold Dorsey's songs on sheet music for ten cents a copy. Many new songs were written expressly for gospel, and black composers found black performers to sing their songs.

The gospel singers performed in churches, in school auditoriums, or wherever they were welcomed. Only in the past few years has black gospel become conspicuous on the national scene. The music was suppressed because the people were suppressed, and with the emergence of the complete emancipation of the Negro has come the emergence of the black gospel song. White audiences are now willing to listen, black audiences have grown with the improvement of the concert facilities and the absence of fear to convene without harassment.

The pathos of the sorrow songs and the classic spirituals lingers in black gospel music. The slave melodies are heard in many songs, reminiscent of past days when a small pleasure was a vast joy, when hope was dared. Gospel music is the black realization of dreams come to pass and their inherent jubilation.

Incorporating jazz and blues into the music, black gospel has been marked with a distinct black beat. Parallel to white gospel again, there are different styles; however, the whole of the music has a distinctive mark which makes each of the songs immediately recognizable as a black gospel as opposed to white. The wild abandon, the shouting quality, and even the body movement brands the music as black.

Today black gospel is performed in concerts, on TV, on radio, and on the numerous records sold. With the recent merger between black gospel and the GMA, it is certain to grow in popularity with black and white listeners alike.

Some of the big names in this type of gospel in the mid-1970s are: James Cleveland, The Swan Silvertones, The Staple Singers, The Caravans, The Five Blind Boys from Alabama, The Harmonizing Four, and Maceo Woods.

The Dove Awards refer to it as "soul," and soul it is, because it comes from the vital depths of a people who did overcome and receive their place in the American dream of freedom and opportunity. From sorrow to shout to soul, black gospel is now a vital part of the American musical tradition.

PART IV
Gospel Music in the Modern World

Chapter 1
GMA: Birth of a Profession

The frock-coated songmaster has evolved into a stylishly dressed businessman, the hammerhead mule has turned into a gleaming Silver Eagle, and gospel music has become not only a profession but a big business.

Quartet managers must concern themselves today with more than concert schedules and song arrangements. It is no longer enough to stand on the running boards and announce the night's performance; promotion is accomplished in all the media and competition is keen. The singers themselves find that they must, as Brock Speer puts it, "wear many hats," and function in many capacities.

Although a big business, it is still not a very lucrative one. The gospel performer's paycheck is only a fraction of the salaries drawn by the rock and country entertainers. Anyone in the gospel field will tell you that while you can earn a pretty good living at the mikes, you are badly fooled if you think that you can make any big money.

The truth is that the glamorous singers seen on stage in well-coiffured hair and flowing chiffon gowns must return home the next Monday to do the family wash and scrub the kitchen floor. The average female gospel performer doesn't go home to a luxurious mansion with a live-in maid and a life of leisure.

Connie Hopper, of the Hopper Brothers and Connie, freely discusses the hardships of road life for the gospel woman. Leaving home Wednesday or Thursday, depending upon how far they will have to travel to reach their first concert date, she and her husband will not return until the late night hours of the following Sunday. In two or three days, the house must be cleaned, the meals cooked and frozen in preparation for her absence, the shopping and laundry done, the errands run, the household bills paid, and the dental appointments kept. She frankly admits the heartache and anxiety that come from leaving her children so often, even though they are well cared for by a relative.

In fact, if you stand backstage and eavesdrop, you will find that the conversation of these gospel ladies is similar to that of any group of mothers and housewives. The talk is mostly of children, recipes, and home. They differ from other women only in the problems of their profession. Their difficulties consist of attempting to press a gown while the bus is going full speed down the interstate; of always being well-groomed and smiling, whether they feel like it or not; and of eating the nearest cafe's hamburger while craving half runner beans, onions, and cornbread. So the question naturally follows: why do it? Admittedly they are not making a fortune, they miss their kids, and standing behind a record rack smiling at the people until two in the morning is only partially relieved by the fact that the curtained table conceals the shoes that have been slipped off. They love it—in capital letters. They love the music, they love the people, and they love the rapport and communication that can only be found when they sing their songs. They hold a common creed, and their conviction is intensified and revitalized when the listeners articulate to them the pleasure and consolation that the gospel singing has brought to them. The giving and sharing between performer and audience make it all worthwhile, and this experience constitutes a love feast of song.

There is a song recently popular, "I'll Go," which embodies the determination of any gospel artist who has endured. Anywhere the people want them, anywhere gospel is welcome, they'll go. It has never been easy; it has not always been pleasant, and sometimes the situation has proven to be much different from what was expected.

Wendy Bagwell's hit of a few years ago, "Here Come the Rattlesnakes," was based on a very real experience. He, with his group, the Sunliters, had been asked to sing at a little church way back up in the hills and hollows. They had never been there before, but accepted the invitation and arrived as planned. During the service, as Wendy, Geri, and Jan were singing some good old foot-stomping gospel, the truth began to emerge. They were in a congregation of snake handlers, and rattlesnakes, alive and hissing, began to appear in the hands of the members. Not wishing to offend anyone, but downright adamant on the point of not touching the tongue-flicking vipers, the group with celerity and dispatch finished their program and made a hasty exit. Wendy's description of the adventure is quite humorous, but certainly the sight of diamondback reptiles mingling among the wires of their electric guitars was not the type of experience gospel singers would usually expect.

Gospel singings are now being held in places which were never considered before. Recent locations have been on aircraft landing strips, on Greyhound tours of mountain greenery, on riverboats, at fairs and Disney-like amusement parks, and aboard ships and planes. The going thing today seems to be the sea cruise or jet flight made with a gospel group to the Caribbean, the Orient, major cities in Europe, or to the Holy Land. Sings are held from the sun-drenched sands of Pacific island beaches to the banks of the Thames, to the entrance of the tomb once owned by Joseph of Arimathea. The gospel groups work with travel agencies in planning these tours and cruises, and the revenue produced from these ventures has become a big portion of their income.

Performers now own or invest in recording studios, record companies, publishing houses, and talent agencies. Some groups such as the Thrashers, Happy Goodmans, Inspirations, Blue Ridge Quartet, Kingsmen, Blackwoods, the Florida Boys, and many more, have their own television shows, some shown nationally, others syndicated.

The Gospel Music Association was formed in 1964 by men in the field with keen minds, progressive thought, and a determination to make gospel music even greater, and who have planned and fostered the expansion and growth of the business. Its officers are elected annually during the National Quartet Convention held in Nashville. From the GMA has come the advent of the Dove, an award for excellence in each area of the field and presented at a banquet held about a month following the convention. The first Doves were given in 1969, the winners being determined by ballots cast by all GMA members. However, in all forthcoming elections only the artists and those actually in the business will have a vote. This is the system used to elect Oscar and Grammy winners.

The GMA is an open-membership organization, and anyone wishing to do so may join on a yearly or lifetime basis. This membership includes a monthly copy of the GMA newsletter, *Good News,* the current GMA Yearbook and Directory, an album of the ten songs nominated for Best Song of the Year, group rates on insurance, admission to the annual meeting, and ballots for the Board of Directors election. Although headquartered in Nashville, the Board meets each month in a different location. Since the Board members pay their own expenses to attend these meetings, an attempt is made to rotate sites in close proximity to the hometowns of the attenders. Not all gospel performers, publishers, and composers home-base in Nashville; in fact, few of them actually do. Rather they live and work in all parts of the country, ranging from Michigan to California and from Texas to New Jersey.

Marvin Norcross, president of Canaan Records in Waco, Texas, was elected in October 1974 as president of the GMA. Its committees were organized and chaired at that time. One of that year's projects was to hold a seminar for the broadcast media in Nashville the first week of July, at which time the International Gospel Song Festival was held, with participants coming from all over the world. Both are now annual events. Looking through the rosters of board members, committee members, and those involved in *Good News* and the Yearbook, it is obvious why Brock Speer said that a gospel man had to wear many hats; they do many jobs. The same names appear in each list.

The entertainers you enjoyed last night spend both travel hours and at-home time forwarding the extension of their industry. It is because of them that gospel music has grown from back-country singing to a profession in evidence around the world.

A Gospel Music Hall of Fame has been established, with W. F. Myers serving as its president. The building is being constructed in Nashville and will house a library, life-size busts of its members, and memorabilia of gospel's past. However, it was decided in 1971 to begin inductions for the Hall, and these have been announced each year at the Dove presentations. In the living category, Jim Waites was the first to enter, and in the deceased, G. T. (Dad) Speer. Other living honorees have included Albert Brumley, Lee Roy Abernathy, and in 1974, James Blackwood. In the deceased category the names entered read like a history of the music itself: Lena Speer, J. D. Vaughan, Adgar M. Pace, John Daniel, Homer Rodeheaver, A. J. Showalter, Frank and Virgil Stamps. Brock Speer, who served for two years as president of the GMA, is now Chairman of the Board for the Hall of Fame and is a trustee of the GMA.

The industry has contributors in differing roles. W. B. Nowlin is one of the largest promoters of gospel concerts in the country, as is Lloyd Orrell. Don

Light was the first gospel music booking agent. Don Light Talent, Inc., was the first to sign the Happy Goodmans and the Oak Ridge Boys, and was also the first to issue musician union contracts. In 1952, Marvin Norcross established Word Records in Waco, Texas. In 1964 Canaan Records, a division of Word, was founded by Norcross and is now the largest publishing and recording concern in the business.

★ ★ ★

Before the last decade, the name Bill Gaither was hardly a household word. He, his wife Gloria, and his brother Danny were traveling the circuits, and at first glance were just a trio with a soft touch approach. Then something happened to set Gaither on a straight and unswerving course which resulted in his name becoming the hottest in the industry.

Gaither wrote a song (he had written others before) that caught the ear of every performer and fan of gospel. "He Touched Me" brought Gaither a Dove in 1969 for Best Songwriter of the Year, an award he has received eight times. In 1974 Gaither was given the Dove for Best Gospel Song of the Year, "Because He Lives," and in 1975 his trio won Best Mixed Gospel Group. In March 1975, he received a gold record from Heartwarming-Impact Recording Co. for having sold over one million albums of his music, the only artist associated with the 12-year-old company to accomplish this feat. He has cut over 20 albums with Gloria and Danny, and if Gaither cuts it, it sells.

A comparatively young man, 42, who has swept a magical wand of success over all that he writes or touches, Gaither has done something perhaps even more outstanding. He has impressed his peers to such an extent that if his name is mentioned to people with names like Speer, Blackwood, LeFevre, or Benson, their opinion is unanimous: "genius." Notable and knowledgeable members of the gospel field respect his talent, believe him to be an excellent musician, and contend that he is writing music that will endure because it is classic. In fact, it is almost a certainty that the mention of the name Gaither will make the praises flow. It would appear that the man not only has no enemies, but that no one is jealous of his success. If this is true, then he is indeed a unique man.

The spring from which this stream of music flows began in 1936 on a farm in Alexandria, Indiana. The Hoosier meadows and fields undulate to the horizon, and a boy grows up listening to the radio, picking up Southern stations projecting Southern gospel music. The lad was intrigued, ordered the songbooks, and learned to sing Brumley, Pace, and Winsett by himself. Later he graduated from Anderson College, and still not leaving the state, received his master's degree from Ball State University, majoring in English and minoring in music. For the few years that he taught, his high school English students never envisioned that this dark-haired, soft-spoken man would one day write songs which would be sung by millions.

What does Gaither say about Gaither? "As Thomas Wolfe said, 'We are all the sum total of our experiences until this minute.'" He believes that college had a great effect on his writing. His wife, Gloria, often helps with the lyrics, and their backgrounds in literature and poetry are certainly contributing influences.

Bill Gaither also fondly remembers camp meeting days and believes that these experiences thread their way into his melodies. Consequently, he sees his music as having both the flavor of the oldtime Southern style and also the impressions that have come from the Northern sacred music.

If he has a message, it is found in the middle ground between getting saved and going to heaven. As Gaither points out, "Between the cross and heaven there's a whole lot of living going on." The Gaithers sing for and about today— how much we can get out of it, what we can do with it.

If he has a motive it is "to make a difference in people's lives." Commenting that a singing should contain both crowd involvement and a spiritual emphasis, he feels that success depends entirely on whether "something spiritually significant happened." He evaluates his own concerts as successful only if he feels "that our being there made a real difference in the lives of those present."

Bill Gaither performs with his wife Gloria and others (brother Danny has now left the group); Henry and Hazel Slaughter are the only other group on the bill. Henry Slaughter won the Dove from 1973 through 1978 as Best Instrumentalist. Henry Slaughter feels that the old all-night sings with five and sometimes six quartets on the bill are soon going to be a thing of the past. As he expressed it, "Once again you have the problem of people getting tired after several hours on a hard seat, and so right in the middle of the group's best number, they get up and walk out." Slaughter believes that "after three hours you can't keep anybody's attention." For a while they tried traveling with one or two other groups, but found that it made the program too long. The two families can give a good evening's program with one intermission for stretching and pizza and cokes. The audience is comfortable, no one moves around, and the performers don't wind up "looking at people's backs," as they begin a song which to them has beauty and merit. As Mr. Slaughter put it, "Sometimes in the old days we had to break piano benches to get the crowd's attention." Well, no one has to bust up the furniture now; the Gaithers and the Slaughters, as indicated by the sell-out concerts, seem to have the problem resolved very well.

If Bill Gaither has a philosophy, it is that "quality makes its own way." He is unruffled by performers in long hair and wired-up amplification. He recently visited a church where he had once taught and directed music. On the evening of his visit, the youthful group, Truth, gave a concert in their own modern style. Their sound must have seemed strange to those who had heard Gaither present Haydn and Beethoven, but the kids were honest and sincere in their attitude, and soon the congregation began to get acquainted with what was going on and to relate to the young sound. Personally, Gaither respects and admires the talents of Andrae Crouch, a modern writer and singer from the West Coast. He certainly accepts the fact that times do change, and while the rock rhythm is not his style, he acknowledges its attraction to many people, and still believes that hard work and talent are prerequisites no matter what kind of music you want to do.

Bill Gaither's songs have been recorded by just about every group in gospel music, as well as by artists in the sacred and popular fields. Some of his most popular songs include "The King is Coming," "There is Just Something About That Name," "Get All Excited," "The Old Rugged Cross Made the

Difference," "Let's Just Praise the Lord," "He Touched Me," "Because He Lives," "I Just Know That Something Good is About to Happen," "Between the Cross and Heaven," "Jesus, We Just Want to Thank You."

Bill Gaither apparently has a long career ahead of him. Today, he is a major influence in gospel music.

★ ★ ★

Indicative of gospel's ability to adapt and conform with the times was the early acceptance of modern hair styles and dress and by the inclusion of a number of instruments not previously used in this music.

Several quartets, composed primarily of young men, completely adopted flared pants and collar-length hair, and sang their gospel with the accent of the new modern composers such as Andrae Crouch. Crouch is a modern touch in and of himself, a Negro man in a field, until recently, comprised solely of whites. Of course, there has always been black gospel music, but the color lines had seldom been crossed. Gene Smith, a veteran of some 40 years in black gospel, entered the white field for some time, but is now semi-retired. The Imperials employed a powerful black singer, Sherman Andrus, who has made his mark, and in time we shall see more of this gospel integration. Crouch, an accomplished performer as well as an excellent writer, fills concert dates all over the country, and has been, at times, joined by Reba Rambo (daughter of Dottie and Buck, the Singing Rambos), providing quite an attraction for the younger audiences.

The Oak Ridge Boys led the way and set the mod-sound pace for other groups to follow with their Dove-winning albums, "Light" and "Street Gospel." The now-generation of these records featured electric guitars, drums, and brass. Other quartets, not wishing to go quite the full distance, have settled for styled hair, nattier suits with white stitching, and a bass guitar.

Yet each group has its own style, and there is something for everyone in gospel music. Those who favor the old-time singing, as it has been sung in the churches, are: the LeFevres, the Happy Goodmans, the Kingsmen, the Inspirations, the Segos, and the Hopper Brothers, and Connie.

Others take a middle-of-the-road approach, singing a few old songs, some with a more modern flavor, and probably some Gaither. These would include: the Speer Family, Thrasher Brothers, the Singing Kolendas, Blackwood Brothers, the Singing Goffs (Mrs. Goff being the former Andrea LeFevre), the Florida Boys, the Blue Ridge, and the Cathedral Quartet.

Brass and up-beat modern are the accents for the Downings, Oak Ridge Boys, Imperials, J. D. Sumner and the Stamps, Danny Lee and the Children of Truth, Sammy Hall Singers, Jake Hess Sound, and Andrae Crouch and the Disciples.

Of course, there are many that are hard to classify. The Rambos have generally a soft approach, leaning on Dottie's lovely melodies. The Lewis Family sings strictly bluegrass, and the Amigos go with a south-of-the-border rhythm. Gaither writes and sings Gaither, and Henry and Hazel Slaughter can sing or play anything. Doug Oldham and Jimmy Swaggart are singles with very distinctive styles. Wendy Bagwell combines comedy with his trio's singing and is known as much for his personality as his music.

There are many groups that have not been mentioned here; to list them all would be a task most difficult. Each has a mode and a method of its own, but each has the same motive—to reach and inspire the audience.

The quartets used varied formats on stage. Many like to have the program lined out and seldom deviate from their planned selections. A few, like the Kingsmen, went on stage without knowing what they might sing. Jim Hamill, for several years the lead, called the shots, and he had a unique talent for knowing just which song was most appropriate for the moment. At times, he would announce a number that the men hadn't done for years, but everybody hung in, and if someone momentarily forgot the lyrics, he just hummed a few bars and later caught up. Hamill is among those who can really talk to an audience and establish a rapport which brings quick response and reaction. His quartet would descend from the stage and stand among the people, singing the songs most requested. James Blackwood has brought this talent of communication with his audience to an art of perfection. Some other performers have attempted this feat and have failed due to lack of talent, or, more often, due to lack of sincerity.

His peers will tell you that Brock Speer has what is probably the most professional group in the industry. He is impressive with his dramatic narratives, and both Brock and Ben, the sound expert, use special effects and sound tracks to maximum advantage in creating mood and atmosphere during their performance.

Singular voices are appreciated for their particular merits. The high notes of Coy Cook rate him as one of the finest tenors in gospel music. Cook is a veteran of many years, having sung with the Dixie Echoes, the Florida Boys, and with London Parris and the Apostles. Coy is almost always introduced to an audience as the "Mayor of Flea Hop." Of course, in reality he isn't a mayor, even assuming that Flea Hop, Alabama, has a mayor. This little town in southeast Alabama is home for Coy Cook, and was given its name through rather unusual circumstances.

The Baptist church in the little village was, in the style of half a century ago, built off the ground and propped and supported by stacks of brick at strategic points, elevating the structure some two or three feet. But one ominous day, two old goats, for reasons known only to themselves, crawled under the church and promptly died. Either their presence was not known or no one cared to haul them out, and so they remained in their hallowed space beneath the flooring of the church. But soon, like rats leaving a sinking ship, the fleas, which had thus far lived among the whiskers and long thick hairs of the goats, left for livelier company. Up through the thin boards they went, and on Sunday morning were lying in wait for the unwary members to convene. Immediately they began finding homes on these new creatures, and the poor church folk, scratching and clawing, were left with no alternative but to make a hasty exit. After much consideration, no solution could be found for the problem, this being before the day of exterminators, and so it was decided that they would simply have to burn down the church. With some kerosene and much reluctance, this was accomplished, and the town built a new church, this one not on stilts. Later someone with a sense of humor gave the little town its name...hence, Mr. Cook of Flea Hop.

Chapter 2
The Record Room

Let the carousel begin spinning,
Let the darkness turn into light.
Hear the gaiety ringing;
It's becoming a special night.

The room was barren, deserted,
Then tables with velvet appeared;
In sequin names they are skirted,
And here the wares are revealed.

Then the records with gay covers wearing,
Stand sentinel on every side.
The colors attack your eyes, tearing;
From its brilliance, you no longer can hide.

Now the room revolves even faster,
The people are filling its space.
Talk rises with laughter,
And the spell, quickly woven, takes place.

In gowns long-flowing and formal,
Hair glistening like sun-drenched sands,
The ladies parade with the pommel
Clutched tightly in ring-fingered hands.

Men strut and pose in their finest,
Lapels of satin and sheen,
Half-boots for gripping the stirrup.
How handsome and gay they all seem.

The Record Room

The music close by is invading,
Its excitement possesses the crowd.
The carousel is now racing,
The riders belonging and proud.

Perfume and pomade intermingle,
With the scent of a jubilee scene,
The thrill of the moment makes tingle
All who hear the joy bells ring.

The vendors are plying their treasure,
Songbook and record and card;
The buyers take each man's measure,
And buy if the soul is unmarred.

The music's tempo is pacing
The riders who spend and who sell.
The whirl has brought them facing
Each other with stories to tell.

The singer gaits with the listener,
The performer keeps step with the fan.
And sharing, there is no visitor,
All are members of a gospel clan.

The young ones are coy and flirty.
The older are suave and aware.
Romance is a muse, not a surety,
But an aura the spell makes so rare.

Sometimes heads are together,
Planning another fair, another day;
While business, it is rather,
An excuse for a longer stay.

The pitch of the song is crescendo,
Faces are a-fire with its blast,
The mark of its beat is an echo,
From the hearts who have felt it at last.

Happiness ticks every moment
From the clock that is moving too fast.
The gathered have shared its foment,
And to its creed, their lot have cast.

Now the carousel is slowing,
The people drift away in regret.
The velvet and sequins are going;
Into cases the records are set.

The spinning has stopped and is still now,
Fair ladies and escorts have gone.
The room is empty and chilled now,
Those who came have sung their last song.

But let the carousel live again!
Let the lights and the colors come back!
In some other town, it will again,
Night after night after night.

—*L.S.B.*

The late afternoon sun's last defiant rays pour through the windshield and bounce off the metallic gleam of the Silver Eagle before it bows low in acquiescence to the west. Its last efforts pick up the tones and hues of the bravado colors that spell the group's name on the flanks of the bus. In convoy lines the Eagles grind to a halt behind the city auditorium. Their coming brings an excitement to the air much like the calliope-led circus parades, and boasts the tingle and tinsel of an opening night anywhere.

Diesel fumes still hang in the air as huge black boxes and cases are pulled from the inner wells of the buses. Then scurrying ants in blue jeans and ski sweaters pick, lift, and carry to a large room adjacent to the auditorium, or into the lobby itself. The big top is going up. Lights are switched on and the black cases are opened to reveal their treasures. Velvet cloths of deep purple and midnight blue are shaken and settled with a flourish over tables which line the walls. Positions of prominence are given the headliners of tonight's bill. Each owner's identity is lettered in sequins and glitter, and the cloths are edged with silver fringe which brushes the floor.

Sentinel racks of wrought iron are erected on either side of the tables and are soon filled with more secrets from the black boxes. Stacks of records, vivid colors behind shining cellophane, are set in their proper places. The busy young ants dig deeper into the treasure chests, and the tables are covered with sheet music and songbooks with shiny new covers, with pendants of wooden crosses pierced with long leather thongs, with glossy photographs of the singers, and with trade papers and publications of the comings and goings of the gospel world.

There is a time limit, a rush to finish before the gates are opened. Then the ants disappear to return as gospel singers and musicians in smartly cut knit suits or tuxedos with ruffled shirts and boots of calfskin or patent leather. The first ticket is sold and the carousel begins to revolve. This is Mardi Gras time for gospel people. Lenten sorrows and the worries of tomorrow are all forgotten for the night. People begin drifting in, and the hum of conversation increases as more enter.

The young girls are usually first. They know the latest fashions, and in high-stacked wedges and pant suits of flowing black silk with cowl collars, whether made from a Simplicity pattern or bought off the rack at J. C. Penney, they add to the luster and aura of glamor that pervades the room. Turtlenecks, leisure suits, and navy suede loafers turn their escorts into handsome princes and contribute to the scene of enchantment. And if they have come unescorted, they giggle in small clusters, sip cokes, and after a few casual turns of the midway, find the conversation of the handsome baritone from Georgia quite fascinating. The crowd expands and the room is soon filled with riders of the merry-go-round evening, costumed in lacy and frilly long dresses of a bygone day, or in navy blazers stitched in red and festooned with shining brass buttons.

Some fans are shy and intimidated, others boldly walk up for an autograph and a brief chat with an admired tenor or bass. The performers are relaxed and friendly, but catch with peripheral vision the fan with the Polaroid and always smile at the appropriate moment. Some of the female vocalists appear, and glamor in vogue reaches its zenith in billowing gowns of chantilly and chiffon or brocades threaded with metallic designs that glisten under the lights. In flawless coiffures and gold evening sandals, they greet the people in a style reminiscent of the elegant ladies of Paris society at their afternoon soirees. Gypsy colors intermingle, and the jingle of earring and bracelet is heard as round and round they go.

It is the showcase for the gospel vendor's wares, the happy hour of sociability, and the fan and performer meet in face-to-face confrontation, and both parties desire it and enjoy it. The conversation is lively, with much repartee and competition of wit. Performer and fan each wish to make a good impression on the other, and they usually succeed in doing so. The long road trips made in weather foul or fair are endured for just this hour, this time when the listener approaches with compliments and words of thanks and encouragement, and the singer, in turn, beams his gratitude, striking the fires of warmth and close affiliation between gospel man and his disciple.

But even with the sincere wish of the gospel entertainer to meet and know his listeners, he is still in business; this is still his livelihood. Bazaars and market-places have always been places of treasure and trivia, of gaily cloaked tradesmen and buyers promenading by the shops, sniffing the offerings and seeking the things that are of worth to them. Such a market, but only for gospel wares, sets its booths and unfurls gay, colored banners and sparkling baubles for the visitors to an evening's sing. The excitement of the vying and competition of the Far East bazaar mantles the once-barren room or lobby of the auditorium. Before and during the concert, there is a constant flow of attenders inspecting the wares, asking questions, and thoroughly enjoying themselves.

Since the gate price for a gospel sing is kept quite low, especially when compared with admission rates for other types of concerts, the gospel singer depends on the sale of his records for a major part of his revenue. The racks stand conspicuously flanking his table and boast gaily colored albums of graphic art or, more usually, portraits of the members of the quartet. After each group's turn on stage, the spokesman announces the bargain sales of the night and promotes their newest album from which they have just done a few numbers.

Tapes are also available, and the success and reception of the quartet that evening is evident if, after the performance, their table is swamped with eager customers. Displayed on the table itself are the many other items of the gospel peddler's goods: wooden crosses from the Holy Land, Bibles, brochures of forthcoming tours and cruises, and GMA Yearbooks are among the items available for the interested shopper. But the important sale is that of the records, mandatory if they are to remain in the black.

During a performance at a church, the placement of albums and accompanying merchandise is left to the discretion of the resident minister. Some will insist that the singers display the items in the entrance hall of the church; others, less inclined toward commercialism, will be respected, and a short announcement is made at the end of the evening that records are offered for sale in the bus. But if the love offering has been small, then the performers earnestly hope that many will choose to come by the bus and make a purchase.

Some singers are criticized for this practice and rebuked for making the commercial announcements, but the complainers don't have any other solution for paying the bill at the local Exxon station, nor would they really believe that the next morning's breakfast could be purchased with a smile and a song. Shades of the old grievances still exist.

★ ★ ★

The record room is a place for friends to meet. Always on the road, good friends may not see each other until both are booked into Electra, Alabama, or Rome, Georgia. Jokes are swapped; compliments are passed, some genuine, some not so real; experiences are shared. There is a catching up with the latest happenings. Baby pictures are pulled out and admired, and mingled in are some bragging and a pinch of gossip.

At times a serious discussion on future plans leads to a business agreement, a change of talent agency, or a record contract. All this may transpire behind a record rack, and the deal made, a handshake is given on the spot. Amid the good-natured kidding and horseplay, decisions may be reached which will affect the entire career of a quartet.

A discontented bass may listen to passing comments and discern whether another group will be needing a new low man soon. If a quartet manager needs a new pianist, a casual stroll between the tables may disclose a veteran ready for a move or a talented and ambitious youngster eager to begin his career.

There is a great deal of camaraderie among gospel people. They, of course, have much in common, experiencing the same pleasures and difficulties of constant travel; all are members of the GMA with everybody knowing everybody else, and, very often, many are related to each other. Here is the common bond found in a minority, and the gospel field has, at least professionally, always been a minority. In the music industry they are outnumbered tenfold by entertainers in pop, country, and rock fields.

Gospel performers have many friends outside the industry, all across the country. As Polly Lewis, of the Lewis Family, once put it, "We are on the road much more than we are at home, so our best friends, rather than being hometown people, are the ones we see as we return with regularity to different cities." Performers and pals now have a chance to chat, and as in days of old when the visiting singing teachers came around, the singers are invited home for pot roast and hospitality. Some groups have fans so loyal that they will travel 100 or more miles to hear their favorites and to see them again.

Unfortunately, not all fans are so kind in their intentions. Dodging and weaving among the admired and the admirers will be found those who are called by gospel people "the spooks," which come in two varieties. There is the spook on the make, the one with a badly written song or a new design for an album cover that he is trying to push. Legitimate sources having failed him, he resorts to an aggressive confrontation with the singers themselves, usually choosing a time when they are either engaged in business or in friendly conversation with a chum. They are tolerated to some degree, ignored as much as possible, and treated with reciprocal rudeness only as a last resort.

The other type of spook is the awe-struck star-worshipper, usually a female, who is so thrilled at her proximity to the object of her admiration that she is effusive in her compliments and comments, and quite often dogs the performer's heels and is irritating in her constant presence. Cloying, and not uncommonly flirtatious, in her approaches to the singer, she can be a source of real embarrassment and discomfort to him. Backstage is frequently the only escape route, and while she sometimes attempts to follow, there is usually a guard at the stage door who will thwart her. Gospel singers refer to the women who follow the bus from town to town as "diesel sniffers." Fortunately there are not too many of these spooks around, but for the performers who have, in the course of doing their jobs, been harassed by the few, the ones that do exist are already too many.

While the record rooms are places of congeniality between the shopkeepers of song and their enthusiasts, backstage is a completely different ballpark, and the frivolities settle down to the serious mien of a profession, but not without its inside humor.

Although many deals are struck beside songbook and record rack, the future of a particular group, and maybe even the future of the field itself, is often affected by the heads close together in discourse by footlight switches or in the privacy of a fire escape. The summer sun setting in hues of rose and gold shadows the faces so rapt with the decisions of gospel's enterprise and extension.

Discord sometimes brings its raised voices and slammed doors. Sad to say, there are promoters who fail to meet the commitment they made concerning the group's salary. This has ever been a nagging thorn in the side of gospel singers. The talent agencies make the bookings with individual promoters and churches, assuming them to be reputable and trustworthy persons. Yet it is not uncommon for a quartet to take its bus halfway across the United States, only to find upon arriving that the church with which they were booked had, in the meantime, sold their contract to another church or organization which had done little, if any, promotion work. The result is a near-empty house, and the singers get only a fraction of their normal salary, sometimes not even enough to cover the expenses of the trip.

While country performers of any name or fame receive five to ten thousand dollars a performance, most gospel groups get, at the most, about 850 dollars, and out of this come the salaries of the eight or nine members, fuel and upkeep of the bus, meals on the road, costumes, and all the other costs entailed in maintaining their sound equipment and other necessary gear. Quartets may find that a promoter has booked them against another major event in the city on the same evening, or he has done a poor job of publicizing the sing, or he has just used poor judgment in speculating the reception of a quartet with a particular style for the city in question.

These promotion mistakes regularly result in a greatly diminished paycheck. At times a firm insistence is required to keep the promoter from taking his cut off the top, before the gate receipts are turned into honestly earned wages. Of course, having once been burned, the performers and the talent agencies keep a list of those not dependable, but new promoters who either welsh or seriously misjudge pop up from time to time. All business is done on a strictly cash basis; it was learned early how many bad checks were given performers, and the court costs incurred, plus the time involved, in attempting to recover the losses of a bouncer, negate the practicality of legal action. Checks are accepted only from old friends and people well known to them.

At the other extreme, some promoters are overly conscious of selling every ticket possible, and keep such tight door security that even the singers them-selves can't get in to perform unless they have a pass or someone at the door recognizes them and will vouch for their identities. At a relaxed sing where there is promoter-performer harmony, the singers' families and a few of their close friends are welcomed in without question, but when dissension reigns, there is no cordiality and the result is often resentment and anger.

But among the singers backstage, horseplay and good humor are frequently the prevailing attitudes. Tale-swapping and practical joking bring laughter from dressing room and stage wing. A proud tenor introduces his lovely new bride around, and the baritone struts proudly with his wife and infant twins, who are interested more in Enfamil and pacifiers than in their daddy's smooth singing.

Jim Hamill, well known lead singer, pads around in stocking feet searching for the brown shoes that match his suit, and giving up the search, still belts some good ones in black loafers. The bass picker retrieves his clean shirt from his guitar case, and all the while Uncle Alph tunes the piano and either Ben Speer or Ray Dean Reese tests, fiddles, and pampers their sound gear.

If Sonny Simmons is tonight's emcee, then he and his clipboard are constantly on the move, and the energy which may have appeared to be wasted evolves into a smooth and well-paced sing.

Wendy Bagwell's bus broke down in Chattanooga, and there is some fast scrambling as Sonny rearranges the line-up. This is generally posted in a conspicuous spot near the stage, and if the Thrasher Brothers or the Stamps aren't due to be on for a while, they take the opportunity to try the concession stand out front for hamburgers and French fries.

The performers watch each other. Most groups have a real respect and admiration for the on-stage entertainers. Sometimes they want to hear a new song which they have heard about, but don't know. And sometimes there is some good-humored fun-poking. It was said one night of a very frightened guitarist that "he was so scared and picking that thing so fast, that he could have threaded a sewing machine while it was running." And if they are especially good friends, the guy in the wings is not beyond a few catcalls and comments designed to break up the men on stage.

If a quartet breaks into a song that is particularly popular with performer and audience alike, there will be a lot of clapping and foot-patting going on. And if a group really gets going, as did the Kingsmen one night in Nashville, then singers will run to the stage from the wings, the audience, or the dressing room, and share the mikes joining in on the fun. Suddenly you will find Ben Speer, Sue Dodge, Willie Wynn, and Coy Cook joining in on "When I Wake Up to Sleep No More."

When Sonny is announcing the next quartet, the singers display various methods of preparing to meet the audience. Ray Reese and Johnny Parrack of the Kingsmen all stand very casually, outwardly cool and poised. Often the facial expression is slightly intense, perhaps betraying the desire to perform and to perform well. Standing behind Coy Cook you see a series of gestures that never varies. First the shoulders are rolled and loosened, the head is twisted slightly from side to side, then the cuffs are pulled down, and the tie and jacket are smoothed and straightened. This done, confidence takes him on stage as "the mayor of Flea Hop" is introduced. Ann Downing clutches the curtain with eager excitement gleaming in her eyes. Smiling across the stage at her husband, Paul, she waits for the call; then they rush with keen anticipation to front and center. James Blackwood often tells his audience, "I've been waiting all night to get out here." This statement is quite believable after seeing him impatiently shift from one foot to the other behind the wing's curtain.

While all performers are enthusiastic when abounding with vitality and good health, the real test comes, as it does for any trouper, when a flu virus is making the head pound and the stomach distinctly unsettled, or when a respiratory infection raises the body temperature to 102 degrees. On those nights of pain or illness, gospel singers come out smiling and put up a facade of well-being. At times they make it by leaning on the piano, sweating hard and singing fast. Occasionally they find that after the first two or three numbers, they can forget their malady and can really join in on the excitement on stage. But if the wisdom tooth aches or the sinus drips, the old adage is remembered and the show goes on. The customers who paid three bucks for their seat will not be disappointed, but after the concert, the stricken singer will fall into his bunk on the bus and wish fervently that he were home instead.

Chapter 3
Motivations and Incentives

Forty years ago the plains of Nebraska, swept by relentless and ever-present winds, stretched past the horizons into infinity. In Tucson, Arizona, there still lingered the scent of sweaty leather, of gunpowder fired in a furious past, of the bitter stench of human fear, and of outlaws, long dead and little grieved. Sophisticated and feigning elegance, Manhattan, bought with worthless chattel, was now part of the city which included Staten Island, the Bronx, and Brooklyn. Springfield, Illinois, immortalized a man who was truly great and who would not have understood the fuss and bother that tourists brought to Lincoln's home. The natives accepted in their midst the long-haired socialist poet Carl Sandburg and wondered if he really thought that he could tell the story of their hero.

All of these places have in common the fact that at this time, gospel music was as unknown and alien to them as were spaceships to the moon. Until the 1930s, gospel songs were a regional phemonenon thriving in the South and parts of the Southwest. The opening strains of "The Eastern Gate" or "On the Jericho Road" would have been strange new sounds for Nebraska's sod-busters and Staten Island's commuters. But this virgin territory was soon invaded by the LeFevres, Blackwoods, Speers, and other pioneers, many of them urged on by the publishing companies. Started in the twenties, held beneath the weight of the thirties, gospel blazed new paths as the forties began with an expansion and an extension that is still in momentum.

During and immediately after the war, many Southerners left cotton field, corn patch, and hill country for the big cities in the North which offered huge factories and plants with well-paid jobs. Some felt the pangs of loneliness in "Detroit City" and came home, but many stayed, relocated Southerners in a situation both urban and strange. They adapted, they adjusted, and tried to cope with the unfamiliar accent and foreign slang of their neighbors. They learned the art of boarding a bus already full and manned by an irascible driver. They tolerated the anonymity of the sidewalks and department stores; they even caught on to the art of dicker and barter with the local butcher and greengrocer.

But they never forgot where they came from, or who they were, or what was their heritage. And if the living room boasted piano or organ, or even a guitar which had once been picked on the back porch of a mountain home, they gathered close in the evenings and sang the old songs learned from childhood.

Imagine their delight when the first gospel group ventured into what might prove to be enemy territory, and renting a hall, announced a gospel sing. Lloyd Orrell, promoter, and The Couriers, singers, were most instrumental in taking the music North. People turned out by the hundreds and left wrapped in nostalgic memories and in the warmth of once-again joining in a jubilee night. They also left begging the singers to return; and return they did. This time the displaced people of gospel took with them friends and neighbors so they, too, could hear the happy sound. To the ears of the newcomers it struck an unfamiliar note, but they came to love the joy-bell music and its exciting singers.

The Reverend George Whitefield, painted by Nathaniel Hone. Courtesy, The Henry Francis
duPont Winterthur Museum.

The foregoing photographs contain the committee appointed by the United Sacred Harp Musical Association in September 1906, who have just completed the revision and compilation and present "Original Sacred Harp" as revised by them. A perusal of its pages will show the work done. Further statements of the corrections in music, additions made, in this valuable song book will be found in the Introductory, by the chairman of the committee, on following pages.

This group picture, which appeared in *Original Sacred Harp*, shows the committee appointed by the United Sacred Harp Association in 1906 to revise the songbook. The fuguing song was written by William Cowper.

Page from *The Easy Instructor*, oldest known shape note songbook. The melody is on the second staff from the bottom. "Old Hundred" was one of the most popular songs in fasola music.

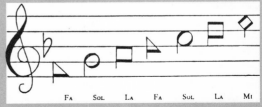

Four shape note sequence used by Little and Smith, published in *The Easy Instructor*.

A copy of the frontispiece of *Harp of Columbia*, first published in 1849 in Knoxville, Tennessee. "Morning Trumpet" was a favorite camp meeting song.

IV

Joseph K. Ruebush, great grandson of Joseph Funk and a relative of Ephraim Ruebush, is shown at a spring near Funk's home in Singer's Glen.

Joseph Funk's home in Singer's Glen, Virginia, shown about 1930; the log building at right was his print shop.

Aldine S. Kieffer.

Seven shape notations. Aiken's, from *The Christian Minstrel*, is still in use, shown here at the top of a list from *White Spirituals in the Southern Uplands*.

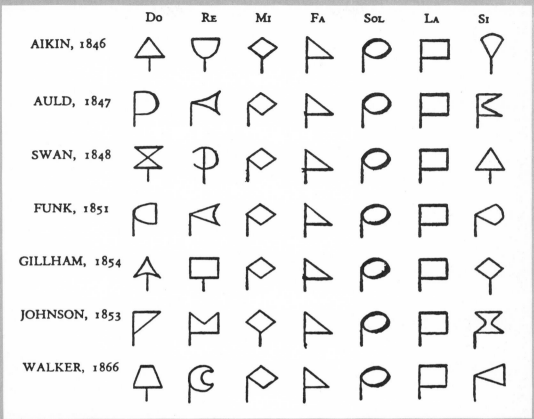

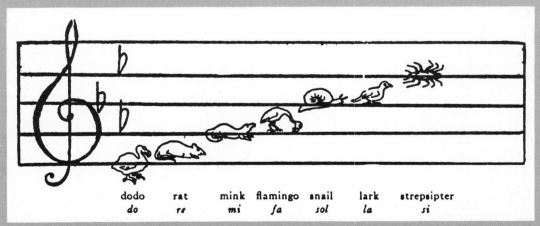

The "Animalistic" scale found in Kieffer's *Musical Million* in 1890 was a joke inspired by an Ohio gentleman.

A. J. Showalter.

J. Henry Showalter, left, a relative of A. J., and George B. Holsinger. Both contributed to shape note singing among the Mennonites.

Benjamin S. Unseld.

V. O. Stamps. Photo courtesy of Stamps-Baxter Music Co.

Stamps Quartet, with V. O. at extreme right. Photo courtesy of Stamps-Baxter Music Co.

Frank Stamps. Photo courtesy of Stamps-Baxter Music Co.

J. R. Baxter. Photo courtesy of Stamps-Baxter Music Company.

Crowd attending a Stamps-Baxter singing school concert on closing night. Courtesy of Stamps-Baxter Music Co.

Stamps-Baxter School of Music, 1948; J. R. Baxter is fourth from left, front row. Photo courtesy of Stamps-Baxter Music Co.

Stamps-Baxter School of Music at Bethel Temple in Dallas, June, 1943. Photo courtesy of Stamps-Baxter Music Co.

R. E. Winsett. Photo courtesy of R. E. Winsett Music Company.

Uncle Alph LeFevre with guitar, Urias, and Eva Mae. Photo courtesy of the LeFevres.

Eva Mae, Urias, and Uncle Alph sporting mustache.
Photo courtesy of the LeFevres.

The LeFevre Trio in the early sixties. Photo courtesy of
the LeFevres.

The Speer Family: Mom and Dad, little Ben between them, Brock on right, sisters Mary Tom and Rosa Nell. Photo courtesy of Brock Speer.

The Speer Family with Ben on left, Brock on right. Photo courtesy of Brock Speer.

A recent picture of the Speer Family with only Brock and Ben from the original group. Photo courtesy of Sumar Talent Agency.

The Cathedral Quartet, winner of the Dove in 1977 for Best Male Gospel Group. Glen Payne stands at extreme left; seated is George Younce, bass. Photo courtesy of Glen Payne.

Wendy Bagwell, left, and the Sunliters. Photo courtesy of Don Light Talent Agency.

The Florida Boys. Les Beasley, manager and lead singer, standing in center, is past president of the Gospel Music Association. Photo courtesy of Don Light Talent Agency.

Les Beasley in the record room. Photo by Lois S. Blackwell.

The Lewis Family, bluegrass gospel singers. Photo courtesy of Don Light Talent Agency.

Rex Nelon Singers with Eva Mae LeFevre, who sings with the group during Atlanta-area performances. Photo courtesy of Don Light Talent Agency.

The Hinsons. Photo courtesy of Don Light Talent Agency.

The Singing Christians. Photo courtesy of Don Light Talent Agency.

James Blackwood.

Blackwood Brothers Quartet in 1955. Back row, from left: pianist Jack Marshall, tenor Bill Shaw, lead James Blackwood. Front row: baritone Cecil Blackwood, bass J. D. Sumner. Photo courtesy of James Blackwood.

James Blackwood, with Tommy Fairchild at piano.

James Blackwood greets a member of the audience. Photo by Lois S. Blackwell.

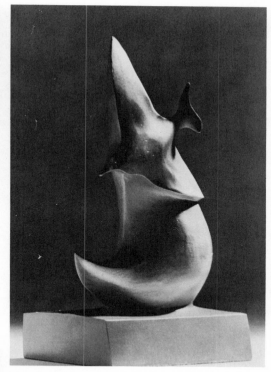

The Gospel Music Association's Dove Award. Photo courtesy of the Gospel Music Association.

Gospel Music Hall of Fame, under construction in 1978. Artist's rendering courtesy of Gospel Music Association.

Statesmen Quartet: Hovie Lister at piano and, from right, bass "Big Chief" Wetherington, baritone Doy Ott, and lead tenor Jim Hill. Photo by Lois S. Blackwell.

Gene Smith, left, was one of the first blacks to enter the predominantly white gospel music field. He is shown here with the late Jim Hill, lead singer for the Statesmen Quartet.

Homecoming at Zion Hill Baptist Church, North Carolina.

Singing at the Zion Hill Homecoming.

TE 1013 PRAISE YE THE LORD, C. C. Stafford (SATB)

Temple
Choral Series
(SATB)
.25

TE 1001	GUIDE MY FEET, J. D. Sumner, arr. Paul Serrin	.25
TE 1002	KEEP ME, J. D. Sumner, arr. Larry Stephens	.25
TE 1003	JESUS, HOLD MY HAND, Albert E. Brumley	.25
TE 1004	JUST A LITTLE WHILE, E. M. Bartlett, arr. Gene Bartlett	.25
TE 1005	LORD, TEACH ME HOW TO PRAY, J. D. Sumner, arr. Gene Bartlett	.25 .25
TE 1006	I KNOW THE LORD HAS LAID HIS HANDS ON ME, arr. Larry Stephens	.25
TE 1007	I WANT TO BE READY, arr. Larry Stephens	.25
TE 1008	MY FAITH LOOKS UP TO THEE, arr. Gene Bartlett	.25
TE 1009	STEAL AWAY, arr. Bob Burroughs	.25
TE 1010	THERE IS A HIGHER POWER, Albert E. Brumley	.25
TE 1011	'TIS SO SWEET TO TRUST IN JESUS, arr. Gene Bartlett	.25
TE 1012	WHITER THAN SNOW, arr. Bob Goodwin	.25
TE 1013	PRAISE YE THE LORD, C. C. Stafford	.25

Front cover of the music for "Praise the Lord" in the Temple Choral Series, C. C. Stafford, publisher, advertises other songs in the series. Courtesy of the late C. C. Stafford.

LeFEVRE SING PUBLISHING COMPANY
P.O. Box 43703
Atlanta, Georgia 30336

Songbook cover, *Songs of Happiness*, courtesy of LeFevre Sing Publishing Company.

As is frequently the case, the young people were the first to go and explore this new sound. Then, once converted, they carried it home for dinner, and their parents, once exposed, extended an invitation to stay over for awhile.

There is, of course, another side to the coin. Many gospel groups went into Northern and mid-Western towns that had no descendants of folk song heritage to lead the way to the ticket gates. They just promoted, prayed, and practiced, and when the doors were opened, people came; whether from simple curiosity or a genuine interest, they came, liked what they heard, and came back.

James Blackwood personally opened the West Coast for gospel music. Going to Pasadena, California, he supervised all promotion work, rented a hall with funds from his own pocket, and visited the churches and talked to the people, some of whom helped with telephone calls announcing his concert. On opening night, the hall was packed, the audience enthralled, and the first inroad for professional gospel was made in a state where others had predicted that gospel music would never catch on. Some years later, Blackwood and his quartet recorded the live album "On Stage," which has become a classic. It was cut in Long Beach, California, and if there was yet a question of an enthusiastic response on the West Coast, that record dispelled it forever.

The whole of the United States, Canada, and many foreign countries have now heard and met gospel's song. The touring quartets tell of warm and stirring welcomes in Europe, Asia, and the islands of the Pacific. Gospel is on the go. Played now on more radio and television stations than ever before, it is beginning to be accepted as a legitimate field of music, unique unto itself, and not merely a fringe of the hillbilly or bluegrass style. It is spreading in every direction, and with its growth comes increasing recognition of its merit and worth. No longer associating it with the tent-packing preachers of dubious veracity or the ribald minority of ranters and rollers, the people of this country and of others acknowledge its dignity, its professionalism, and its inspirational attributes. In a world of negativism and discontent, its accent on optimism and its positive approach win the admiration of those who once felt that it belonged only in a back country church. Many accept its emphasis, others wholly endorse its purpose, and a number adhere completely to its fundamental creed. The ripe years of maturity have come to gospel, and as the world watches, it sings the songs born in kindred hearts more than 200 years ago; and while it has progressed, grown, and seasoned, it has not relinquished that first flush of freedom of the advent of a music conceived in the heart and retaining the strains and the faith of those who first sang it by torch fire and in moon-filled clearings.

There is a song written by Nancy Harmon, sung by the LeFevres and other groups, which tells the whole story of these gospel people, and why they are willing to grind out the endless miles, eat the Blue Plate specials, and contend with the low salaries of their profession. If it is not for the money, and if it is not for personal acclaim, which they seldom receive except occasionally from their peers, then what is their compulsion, their motive, their reason for choosing this life? This song is the testimony of every gospel singer who is true to himself and to his audience:

I'll Go

If you need a voice to speak for You, I'll speak, Lord, I'll speak,
If you need someone to weep for souls, I'll weep, Lord, I'll weep;
If I see You've got a job to do, then I'll work, Lord, anytime for you,
Tho it may be morning, night, or noon, I'll go, Lord, I'll go.

I'll go, I'll go! Anytime, any place, to any creature of any race;
To the mountains, thru the valley, cross the river, thru heat or cold,
Anywhere you lead me, Lord, I'll go!
I'll go, I'll go, I'll go!

Eva Mae LeFevre, the great lady of gospel music, who has been on the road for over 40 years with husband Urias and Uncle Alph, often speaks of those early days when crossing the valleys and the rivers was not so easily done. She recounts the times when Urias and Alph resolved the problem of a river crossing by undressing and holding instruments and clothing high over their heads as they waded or swam across. This, of course, was in sparsely settled country, and what the kids consider fun today and call skinny-dipping, was not quite such a treat when March winds were blowing and the water was as cold as only mountain heading waters can be. But upon reaching the other side, they shook themselves like wet retrievers, and after redressing, continued their walk to the singing over the hill. They and others like them have known the heat and the cold, the earthly valleys of the alternating season's eccentricities of weather, and the spiritual valleys of despair, discouragement, and disappointment.

The veterans say that it is quickly discernible whether a new quartet has begun their career with a sincere dedication or with hopes for a flashy, glamorized means of earning a living. Those who are out for the fast buck, or some feminine attention attracted by their crushed velvet jackets, fall by the wayside. The hours are too long, the work too demanding, and the pay much less than anticipated. It takes a firm conviction and a total belief in the merit of what they might accomplish to keep the bus tires rolling down the freeways and across the ridges to city auditorium and small town church.

Looking at a month's concert schedule for many of the groups, especially the older ones whose careers began on the Sunday School circuit, you will find that they book as many churches with names like Mt. Moriah or Ebenezer or Macedonia as they contract to sing in big town halls and city civic centers. They consider it their job to sing to the people, all of the people. Actually, the full concert given at Green River Church is frequently more spiritually satisfying to them than a performance at a municipal hall or at a steeple-topped brick building of huge dimensions and vast congregation.

It has been reported that many times the cushioned pews extending back in countless rows contain the urbanized and self-conscious who deem it unseemly and unsophisticated to react or respond to the music, and so sit stiffly without trace of smile or enjoyment. It is certainly difficult for any entertainer to sing to a cold audience, and, if anything, it is even more demanding for the gospel singer, who is there expressly to share his happiness and zeal for God's gifts of life and love. On the Kingsmen's Dove-winning album, "Big and Live," Jim Hamill describes such a congregation as "looking like they were baptized in vinegar, weaned on a dill pickle, and born on the wrong side of the moon."

The smaller crowds at Bent Creek and Mt. Pleasant have no shyness in exhibiting their enjoyment and appreciation of the singers' efforts. The pay for the evening may only be the love offering collected by the ushers, but the people articulate their delight and vocalize their gratification for the music. An older gentleman in one of these little churches was once heard to comment, when the name James Blackwood came up, "Why, I've been a-knowing James for a long time." Like the traveling singing master of bygone days, the modern gospel singer still has and keeps a very personal contact with his listeners. As the song says, they "speak" to the people and "weep" with them for their sorrows or stories of distress. The man laden with problems or worries will take his troubles to one whom he knows will be of similar belief and persuasion. He finds the kind word, the understanding sympathy, and the handclasp of genuine concern.

Happiness is as quickly shared, and the situation is one of friendliness and empathy rather than the relationship of aloof star and admiring fan. This cordiality is not true of every gospel performer, for there are always sheep and some goats, but the goats are usually easy to spot and they probably won't be around long anyway.

And so they go—with good will and with relish and gusto. And in the attitude of a young lady still in her twenties, we find the future of gospel music: "Sometimes the work is tiring, but it is never tiresome." In many of these youthful people has been kindled the spark that put the old quartets on rocky roads in cars of intractable transmission and contrary carburetor. The dove flies for them too, and they have taken the vow to go "anytime, any place" singing the gospel song.

Most of the more established groups have taken the inexperienced youths into their circle, and have provided them with advanced musical training, experienced advice, and encouragement for their fine efforts. Other youngsters have started on their own, and one group, the Higher Ground, is receiving rave reviews wherever they sing. The offspring of the veterans are many times found singing or playing during summer vacations and school holidays, and will, after graduation, go full time on the road. The sons of Ben Speer, James Blackwood, Coy Cook, Tommy Fairchild, and Connie and Claude Hopper are some of the second-generation performers.

Countless nephews, daughters, and nieces may not appear on stage, but work in the family business as sound engineers, secretaries, or composers and arrangers. A large number are active in the GMA and serve in various capacities. Some write for the tradepapers or work in public relations with disc jockeys and talent agencies.

The smooth-faced and frosty-haired singers on today's stage will still be up there in years to come, a little more matured, perhaps a little more poised, but unchanged in their personal dedication and promise "to go." The music may be a bit different. Gone will be the distinct flavor and spice of the music of those who endured the physical hardships, the labor of laying the foundation for a profession, the experiences of those who dined on pork and bean and onion sandwiches when the purse proved empty.

What new bricks the young people will add to a structure cemented with honest sweat, shaped by hands that have ached in cold and weariness, and founded on the stones of devotion can not yet be imagined. But add they will, for in zealous enthusiasm they are most certainly activists, and will not permit stagnation nor neglect. That which they bring forth may seem at first, to those of riper age, a little odd, maybe even a little revolutionary. But raised in the gospel heritage, they will contribute, never diminish nor lessen, and their additions to the field will act as sun and rain to seed, and gospel will continue to develop and to grow even stronger. With them is gospel music's future, and the forecast looks bright into years of progress and development.

Part V
The Reason For It All

Marshall McLuhan, Director of the Center for Culture and Technology at the University of Toronto and possessor of a Ph.D. from Cambridge University, has written several books, among them, the controversial *Understanding Media*, in which he discusses the effects of electronic communication on our modern world. Here he presents his famous one-liner "the medium is the message." He defines this phrase to mean that it is not the programing presented on television or radio that contains the message or point to be made, rather the tubes and electric components comprise the message now being received by the people of the twentieth century.

He explains that the instantaneousness of electricity which allows the entire globe to witness the death of an American President, a space landing, or the Olympic games draws the world closer and reduces scattered tribes on widespread continents into a closer-knit universal community. This action, of course, makes us more aware and conscious of the problems and needs of people once far removed from us. The message here is that, as John Donne once put it, "No man is an island, entire unto himself." Technology has drawn us into an involvement and a confrontation which invites, even insists upon, an empathy which has never existed before.

Dr. McLuhan classifies media in two forms, hot and cool. The hot media are those which create no need for involvement, do not affect our senses, and are out of step with today's world. He lists movies, much of the printed media, and radio as hot since they require no participation from the people and leave no empty spaces for us to fill in. But cool media require total involvement, affect all our senses, demand participation, and give opportunity for our minds, imaginations, and innermost feelings to have freedom and room for expression.

If we use Dr. McLuhan's definitions, then gospel music is surely among the coolest media in existence today. In a country which has seen the congeniality and common sharing of the pioneers, watched country descendants turning to aloof anonymity through urbanization, mutual distrust and a reduction of human compassion, involvement has become a dirty word and is more avoided than the plague victims of another century.

Society has dispersed itself into separate entities and pockets of self-sustaining organizations and groups which help only those of their particular choice and affiliate and align themselves with no one alien to their tight little bands. The rule of the day is don't associate with the outsiders, meaning anyone outside the imaginary periphery of geographical, ethnic, social, religious, and economic boundaries.

Donne said, "Each man's death diminishes me, for I am involved in mankind." How far many of the people in this country have gone from that philosophy! Yet, there has always been one clan of disciples which has held Donne's truth as a basic tenet in its creed, and has for over two centuries extended the out-stretched hand of compassion and invitation.

The singers of the gospel song created their music from a very real need for involvement and commitment with a viable and loving God, and with this commitment came the extension of participation offered to any who wished to join in the hallelujah song. For this reason gospel music stands unique in the pages of history and remains today as the only form of music which encourages its sharing and which is sung for the total purpose of involving singer and listener in a mutual experience of joy and a joint expression of kindred feelings and happiness expounded in a communion of song.

This music answers each of McLuhan's requirements for a cool medium, which he says the world needs today. As we have seen, the performers journey the distance to reach the people, and once there, attempt with all the talent and vitality they possess to sing out the glad note with an open invitation for the audience to share their cheerful enthusiasm and become involved with their message. Their medium is their message, the music itself, the kindred song of gospel.

Gospel music invades and stimulates all our senses, except perhaps the tactile, which becomes included with the hand-clapping and foot-tapping that accompanies the lively song. Eyes reflect the presence and countenance of the singers, and the beaming faces in animation disclose dispositions and attitudes of zest. The audio system is penetrated, sometimes soothingly, sometimes with a pulsating vibration that arouses and excites.

And what is in the air? The adrenal ejections of throbbing heartbeats and accelerated metabolism cloud over cologne and cosmetic bouquet. The metallic aroma from the electric instruments and the scent of many human beings confined in one space and place permeate the nostrils. Oral gratification comes in several ways. The audience is often invited to sing along on well-known songs, and frequently without explicit permission, many sing softly to themselves the chorus that has special significance for them. The older folks, accustomed to such practices on Sunday morning, will at times exclaim in appreciation and joyfulness a good old-fashioned "hallelujah" or "amen."

As for McLuhan's third prerequisite, there would be no gospel music without participation. As we have seen, gospel's first principle is the sharing of God's grace with God's people. Music is not a sacrament, and yet the people come to partake of a communion of song and the musical altar is one which solicits participation.

There may be a great urge at a Beethoven concert to jump up and say "right on" or "amen" or something appropriate to the moment, but the problem is that nothing of that sort is appropriate. Van Cliburn bows stiffly from the waist and proceeds to play his concertos; his Rachmaninoff can make you weep and his Mozart is a thing of beauty you wish to touch, but any audible display of appreciation would merit you a fast exit by an irate usher who would think you some kind of a nut. Neither the magnificence of a contralto's voice nor the easy identification with Johnny Cash's lyrics provides excuse or opportunity to react and respond, except with the applause of an isolated listener. Surely, the primary characteristic of gospel music is that it does, as it always has, invite participation and urge its listeners to join in the joy of its performance.

Gospel songs all have much the same theme, but are still deeply personal and individualized since each person has his own dreams of Zion and his own visions of his mansions and walls of jasper. Also, there is enough generalization in many of the songs that, although retaining a story line common to all, there is enough space between the lines for everyone to make a personal application. A song revived and once more popular, "Love Will Roll the Clouds Away," contains the simple theme and single message characteristic of gospel, that although we may be beset with troubles today, the time will indeed come when the clouds will be gone and "the darkness will turn to day." Each man and woman can apply a distinct and personal interpretation to this theme.

Another current favorite is "When I Wake Up to Sleep No More," with its promise of a different morning, a new day. It expresses the happiness of that time yet to come, but since no one knows exactly what that dawning will be like, each listener can preceive his own vision of just how it will be.

Since the Puritan children broke with the church of their fathers and began their search for a live and communicative God, their music and the music of their descendants has contained the bridge from man to Maker and from neighbor to stranger. The communion that springs from the clasp of hands and from the rearrangement of the lines of age and worry to produce the glad smile, speak of the involvement that gospel can bring. To emote in a technocratic world is often to become suspect. The expected and accepted form of behavior is an objective and detatched aloofness. But in gospel music lies a standing opportunity, socially acceptable, to express affection and love, and to display emotions that under other conditions would probably appear naive or uncouth, even corny.

The great attraction of gospel music for many young people was mentioned earlier. This interest is based on the sympathy of today's youth toward freedom of expression; they prefer to be in a position of inclusion. In *The Making of a Counter Culture*, Theodore Roszak discusses modern man's feelings of alienation in our world, with many references to the philosopher Marcuse and his theories. Through the years, man's deliberate, and perhaps sometimes unplanned, withdrawal into his self-contained sphere (looking out with objectivity and fearing involvement) has created alienation from the world, from those around him, and even from himself. He is part of no one and nothing.

Today's young adults reject alienation. They seek communion with the human race; they welcome personal experience, the gratification of vocalizing their fears and dreams, and a free expression.

Some, of course, grew up with gospel, and it is as familiar to them as the breeze-ruffled chintz curtains in their rooms at home. But many were led to gospel by friends or dates. They liked what they saw and felt—the open welcome of performer and fan, the congress of mutual emotions that convened under the music. Nothing turns off youth as does negativism, and gospel turns them on with the pure optimism and complete hope embraced in its songs and its singers. They once called a spontaneous experience a "happening." The word seems to be passe now, but this is still what they are seeking: an event that brings joy, yet has for them merit and worth and meaning. The real, the honest, and the basic are venerated by those who despise the plastic and artificial. They recognize gospel people as very real and down-to-earth. They can spot the sellers of snake oil, and you won't see any of the ones who have it all together hanging around the modern-day medicine shows. Reality and basics, and the chance to express glad feelings from the floodgate of their vitality and exuberance are reasons why the under-25 crowd pushes the turnstiles at a gospel sing.

At the National Quartet Convention in October 1974, over half the audience was under 30 years of age. "Get All Excited" says a gospel song, and they do. They clap and sing and have a great time. There are no drugs, no chemically-induced trips. They don't need them, and they aren't the right candidates for that type of venture anyway. They can smile, laugh, weep, or embrace a friend just because they are happy, and there is no fear of castigation. It is an outlet, a hope, and for many, a creed and a way of life. As long as youth can find expression and involvement, love and reality in gospel music, then its future seems endless and in good hands.

Many churches today do not offer their members any chance for participation in the services. The minister conducts and carries the whole hour, and the people are permitted only certain responses prescribed by the usual ceremony. This is most particularly true of the liturgical churches, but is also true in many other congregations of varying denominations. In a Lutheran church a couple of years ago, the pastor decided that he would make an attempt to draw his members into a closer communion of worship. In the service is found a blessing which the minister gives to the congregation, "The Lord be with you," to which the people respond, "And with thy spirit." On this particular morning, the pastor announced that beginning at the left front pew, the end person would turn to the one standing on his left and greet him with "The Lord be with you," clasping his hand in fellowship. That person was then to answer with the usual response, "And with thy spirit," then turn to the person on his left and continue until each member assembled would have offered and received this blessing with his fellow communers.

The members were a little embarrassed at this deviation from the norm and at the sudden vocal role they were asked to play. But as the initial strangeness abated, they broke into smiles and enjoyed what was for them a novel experience. Perhaps if more pastors were innovative and started incorporating their members into personal involvement into the services, their pews would begin filling and their attendance rate increase.

Young people definitely do not like to be "talked at," or to be required to sing the same hymns every Sunday. This is evident in any church where one Sunday a year is allocated as Youth Sunday and the youngsters are allowed to conduct the morning's worship themselves. Such a service provides each young person in the church with a role; no one is ever left out, and new religious songs which are reverent and inspiring in theme, but livelier and more spirited in tempo are mimeographed and passed by the ushers. When these young adults cannot find the opportunity to participate in their church's services and programs, many of them turn to gospel music for its message, its warmth, and its accent on inclusion of all, exclusion of none.

Youth can and does speak to youth. Many gospel groups are composed almost solely of members of the "now" generation: The Blackwood Singers, the Higher Ground, the Regents, the Tribunes, the Archers, the Young Deacons, and Danny Lee and the Children of Truth.

The Singing Kolenda Family has Mom in the wings and Dad playing guitar and as spokesman for the group, but the singers are sisters Cheryl, Linda, and Karen, and brother Arnie. All in their twenties, they are attuned to the drummer's beat of the generation born in the fifties.

For the city-dweller in Connecticut or Milwaukee, to whom gospel is still alien and who is not on speaking terms with his neighbor in the next apartment, all of this get-together talk of hand-clapping and foot-tapping in gladness created by the music, must sound strange indeed. But people are no different now than when they began to gather in small bands for herd-like protection and a shielding from the terrors of the night.

People still need each other, no matter what their religion or lack of it. Perhaps in gospel music they can find once again the ability to let down their fences and share their feelings and emotions with others made in the same image. It is a cliche to say that to share is to be enriched, but it is often repeated because it is true and always has been true. Our youth know this and lead the way in discovering themselves and each other, and sometimes even a way of life.

Computers are sterile and lifeless, having no love to give nor the capacity to receive it, but man is not a machine and is capable of both giving and receiving. Gospel music is involvement, and for that reason has endured for over two centuries, and from the actions and intentions of youth—both singers and listeners—it will be sung for centuries to come.

Part VI
Gospel Today: The Result of Two Decades

A nation at war turns to its God, and the residual effects may remain for some time. Although this country is an amalgamation of many nationalities and creeds, we suddenly became a Christian nation. Between 1940 and 1958, church attendance in the United States increased from 64.5 to 109.6 million. Religion showed its face in places never before seen.

Beginning in the 1950s, the President opened his Cabinet meetings with prayer, and special rooms were designated as places for prayer and meditation at the Capitol building and at the United Nations. "Under God" was added to the pledge of allegiance to the flag. Businesses of different kinds now started each working day with a morning prayer, and organizations of "Christian business-men" sprang up across the country. Billy Graham held meetings, mass meetings, and finally crusades to save the sinners. As was noted before, the schools during the war years had begun to hold morning devotions, a practice which continued until a declared atheist created a furor, and Congress declared it unlawful to impose Christian services upon students of varying religions.

Religious songs were now found on the Hit Parade, and religion-oriented books became bestsellers. Rabbi Joshua Loth Liebman's *Peace of Mind* came out in 1946, and Bishop Fulton J. Sheen's *Peace of Soul* followed in 1949. Norman Vincent Peale produced *The Power of Positive Thinking* in 1952, the Protestant answer to negativism. From *The National Experience: Part II* comes this comment: "The new, nondoctrinal faith seemed designated to dispel anxiety, to induce self-confidence and even self-righteousness, to guarantee success for the individual in his professional career and victory for the nation in its struggle against atheistic, materialistic communism. Religious affiliation seemed to provide a means by which Americans could define themselves in their community and their society. Religion became part of 'belonging,' a quick way to establish a social identity."

First there was a Great Awakening, a Second Awakening, and now the American people found themselves enmeshed in a non-theological awakening. The post-war years brought the first pangs of alienation to a society which heretofore had either lived in rural settings, small towns, or fairly intimate circles in the bigger cities. The technocratic age had begun, and no longer was your face or name important; the American had become a number. To his bank, to his charge accounts, in the hospitals, from his book-of-the-month-club to his private physician, he was no more an individual; he was his account number or his identification number. The person was non-existent. Jobs stole identity as men and women whose forebears had been known for their personal skill or talent now were mere links in chains of industrial lines, steno pools, and working crews. If a person wasn't known for his work and he had no prodigious talent to take him above the ranks of the average, then he was simply one of the "little people" who must function if the businesses and industries of the nation were to continue. Yet, as an individual, who was he? No one seemed to care.

The young people of the fifties attempted to solve this problem of alienation with a grasping hold to conformity. Girls grew up expecting to find the "right guy," marry, have children, and establish the family unit. Boys sought the girls who would make proper wives by raising their children, entertaining their clients, and becoming impeccable housewives. Meanwhile, they pursued careers in respectable areas: law, business, medicine, and education. The youth portrayed in the TV program "Happy Days" have been called by sociologists "the silent generation": Don't muddy the waters, don't buck city hall; just take your kids to Sunday School and keep your nose clean. They felt that they were doing what was expected of the average American family, and how could alienation touch you if you were squeaky clean?

In *The Caine Mutiny*, a book by Herman Wouk popular in the 1950s, the antagonist was the young lieutenant who challenged the unreasonable, irrational captain. This philosophy came during a period in which people were trained not to question authority or the organization. Yet, under the superficial calm were those who questioned the validity of keeping quiet. J. D. Salinger's *Catcher in the Rye,* Mary McCarthy's *The Group,* and the plays of Tennessee Williams and Arthur Miller were addressed to the problem of personal identity. Platitudes didn't quite fill the bill, and many minds, both great and small, were searching for answers.

Observers of the social scene began to write and more people began to read. Between 1952 and 1961, the paperback book business increased 150 percent. Culture, in whatever form, boomed, and Americans now had the opportunity to choose between pop art, expressionism, and the old classics. The sixties burst forth with innovative ideas and inane attempts to be different; no longer was the norm to be tolerated. The beatniks put down "the establishment" with their bored existentialism. Mort Sahl was one of the first to introduce black humor and sick jokes. The purpose seemed to be negative appraisals of anyone and everyone, including oneself.

John F. Kennedy, in 1961, criticized the fifties and presented himself to the people as a youthful man full of zest for living, an appreciation for the arts, and with a positive approach the White House had not experienced for some time. Marshall McLuhan had begun his reflections on the pros and cons of an electronic age of communication on a global basis. Dr. Reinhold Neibuhr of Union Theological Seminary was one of the leaders who sought to make the Christian faith relevant and alive in the mid-twentieth century. Where Dr. Peale and many of his associates had turned a doctrinal faith into a philosophy compatible with the current values in American society, Dr. Niebuhr stressed the individual experience and the twenty-fifth chapter of Matthew, which precludes that man is indeed his brother's keeper. Niebuhr and his colleagues sparked a new breed of ministers who concerned themselves with the issues of the day: civil rights, tenants' councils, welfare unions, and rent wars in the slums.

The activist clergy and the influence of President Kennedy caused the young people in the nation to become aware of the plight of the less fortunate and the abused. VISTA and the Peace Corps were formed and continue to operate. College campuses made the front pages with their fights against prejudice and unfair treatment. Students became interested in politics and concerned about more substantive issues. The Students for a Democratic Society (SDS) was formed and became a powerful influence among many college students. However, many young people carried the New Frontier's philosophies beyond reasonable bounds. Kennedy's assassination underlined the younger generation's distrust of contemporary values and motives; the older generation was rejected, along with its sense of order and propriety. In 1965 from the University of California came the new slogan: "You can't trust anyone over thirty." Going to the extreme, American youth decided that only they knew what was honest and true.

They were putting into words and actions what the "beat" generation of the late fifties had insinuated in their poems, jazz music, and their identification with the rebellious movie stars James Dean and Marlon Brando. They had been "rebels without a cause," distrustful of existing ethics, but with no definite goal toward which to work. They had gathered in San Francisco and New Orleans for the most part, and expressed their alienation from the older generation with a new language all their own. The new vocabulary of "cool" and "jive" set them apart, they felt, from the straights, the squares who "dug on" society as it existed.

Then the hippies of the sixties took the stage. They were often not the intellectual peers of their beatnik predecessors. They came from all classes, runaways from affluence and survivors from the street. For the most part, they reflected what America considered as lower class. They defied convention with long hair and beards, paraphernalia dress, bare feet, and an apparent contempt for hygiene. Haight-Ashbury in San Francisco and Sunset Strip, along with the ever-Bohemian east side of New York, begot the hippie. Crime increased, and most of the arrests in this period were of kids, 15 years old or even younger.

The Viet Nam doves fled to Canada and defected from American society and a war they didn't create. A nationwide debate continues on the subject of amnesty for the draft-dodgers. The Black Panthers chose violence as the solution to their problems. However, the big problem came in pills, packets, and rolls as many young people sought to surfeit every sense with the deafening sounds of acid rock and the highs and lows of various pills and drugs. LSD was a psychedelic answer as the strobe lights spun and the stereos blasted with bass guitar and drums.

The age of assassinations had begun: TV switched from Westerns to situation comedies which ran the gamut from "The Dick Van Dyke Show" to the absurdity of "The Beverly Hillbillies," and ecumenism was again being touted as the answer to the problems of the organized church.

Betty Friedan wrote a book, *The Feminine Mystique,* which became the Bible for the women's lib movement and Ms. Friedan was considered the modern progenitor of the call to "free the enslaved female." American social problems were attacked by the Job Corps for men and women, and it was the time for volunteer work to solve the problem of the neglected youngster, the working wife, and last, but certainly not least, the racial issue. Lyndon Johnson approved bussing while black children were harassed if they visited friends who were white and lived in a white neighborhood. The laws had been passed, but enforcing them was another question. Private schools sprang up all over the South, particularly parochial schools where Christian parents could send their children without fear that they would have to sit next to a black child in the classroom.

However, the youths took the stage front and center. Merchants were among the first to recognize this fact, and marketing was soon directed at those under 20. Plastic was the cardinal sin and the unspeakable word, and the young people who decried the false and mercenary values of their parents spent millions on health foods, transistor radios, camping vans, and rock music. Convention was denied, even mocked. School dress codes were defied, even unto court cases. Runaways reached an all-time high among kids who thought that their parents cared more for their cocktail parties and new cars than for freedom of expression for their offspring. Psychologists had a field day telling distraught mamas and daddies how they had suppressed their child's need for self-development and uncontrolled flights into their justified fantasies. Rock festivals began, as did "understandings" between couples who lived together for awhile to see if they could make it in marriage, or just because they wanted to. Movies were no longer simple matters. No one must check the rating, and anything beyond a "G" was sure to contain something that the Roy Rogers westerns or the Gene Kelly musicals would have blushed to see or hear. Porno shops began to proliferate, and behind them came the massage parlors. It all made the hootchie-kootchie show of the county fairs seem like Disneyland on parade.

A religious bomb was dropped in the mid-sixties with the explosive catch-phrase "God is dead." One of the main figures in the controversial and much-misunderstood issue was Thomas J. J. Altizer, who at that time was a professor in the religion department at Emory University.

Theodore H. Runyon, Acting Associate Dean of the Candler School of Theology at Emory gives, in a letter to this author, the following interpretation of Altizer's philosophy: "Altizer's theology was that God has chosen to identify so completely with the world that he has merged with the world. This is the inner meaning of the cross (cf. Philippians 2:7 and 8), and therefore Christians must now find God in the world with which Christ has merged himself in his death. God is not to be found in some distant heaven, therefore, but in the world."

The passage to which Dr. Runyon refers is as follows:

Philippians, Chapter 2, Verses 7 and 8: But made himself of no reputation, and took upon him the form of a servant, and was made in the likeness of men. And being found in fashion as a man, he humbled himself, and became obedient unto death, even the death of the cross.

Altizer and his colleagues who expounded this thesis were proclaimed atheists by the fundamentalists. They interpreted the statement to mean that the theologians felt that God no longer existed as a Divine Being. They thought that the actuality of a real Presence was being questioned. The Bible Belt thought that the fact of a live and vital God had been denied, and they retaliated by slogans such as, "God isn't dead, I talked to Him this morning."

A gospel song was written to disprove Altizer's thesis. "If God is Dead, Who's That Living in My Soul?" became a popular song among the dissenters. The lyrics were an attempt to describe the effects that a viable God had upon their lives.

> He gives them shelter from life's stormy weather.
> Gives them love to keep them together;
> And when the stage of life grows cold,
> Somebody helps us play our role....
> If God is dead, then who's that living in my soul?
> If my soul had windows, I'd leave them open so the world could see
> The ugly scars upon those hands that bled for you and me.
> If God is dead, then Who's that living in my soul?

> —*L. Reynolds*

The point that Thomas J. J. Altizer and those who agreed with him were attempting to make was that the alienation of God from man and of man from man was the real enemy. The technocratic age had spawned alienation, and the theologians were trying to find an answer for Christians living in that age. While Dean Runyon did not agree entirely with the "God is dead" statement, he did comment in a lecture at Emory University on February 13, 1966, later published in *The Death of God Debate* and reprinted in *The Theology of Altizer: Critique and Response:* "With this one act of self-giving, namely, the life and death of Jesus Christ, God willed to join Himself with the world, so that from henceforth He is no longer to be found in the heavens—the transcendent, domineering God is dead—but must be found where He wills to be found, that is, in His world."

Thus Dean Runyon suggested that God was not an unreachable overlord, but rather, a Presence who lived with and in the people. On the problem of man's alienation from man, Dean Runyon has this to say in the same lecture. "This is precisely modern man's problem. He no longer has a context within which to understand his life as responsible to anyone but himself....But I am convinced that only by this kind (the God is dead debate) of open-ended research can we hope to begin to answer the challenges which theology faces today and arrive at a new language—or new languages—which can mediate to man once again full, human existence, which is the goal we are all seeking."

As happens with all such religious arguments, the ferment and furor eventually abated and other issues took the center stage. Old quarrels continued, such as the repudiation of the Revised Standard Version of the Bible and its reference to Mary, mother of Christ, as "young woman" and not "virgin." The fundamentalist's acceptance of TV and movies caused violent disputes, and the dissent goes on among the various sects as to the sinfulness of make-up, shorts, and dancing. Each decade brings its theological debate, which usually dies out before it is settled in any definitive way. However, in most cases there is some good to come from each dissention.

Dean Runyon made this comment in 1977: "Nevertheless the controversy did have the salutary effect of forcing people to think about how real (or non-real) God was for them, and the end result may have been the revitalizing of faith for many."

★ ★ ★

In the early 1960s folk music was all the rage. The young people, boys and girls alike, wore blue jeans, hang-tail sloppy shirts, and long, long hair as they listened to Joan Baez, Bob Dylan, Peter, Paul, and Mary, the Kingston Trio, and soon after, Sonny and Cher. The youth in America had made themselves prominent on the national scene with their "down with the establishment, back to basics" philosophy. From their primary interest in what was natural in food, clothing, lifestyle, and attitude, evolved communes, pot parties, and sexual permissiveness as the order of the day.

Then in the middle of all this permissiveness, came a brand of young people who said, "I don't like what I see. What else is around besides the pot, pills, and anti-moral, anti-parental teachings?" Fearing the bomb, the Viet Nam war, and the dehumanizing trend in the American scene, a small minority began preaching, "Make love, not war"; these "flower children" begot the love-ins, the happenings. The number was small, but the ranks grew slowly. From the first love child came the first young person who decided that something other than mind-stifling drugs and a purposeless existence must be available.

The Jesus people were called freaks, and some were, but soon a new type of youth emerged who focused on the Christian faith as the definite solution to the problems of the day, not merely another trip to be tried. Out of the newness and turmoil came something of substance, something with which the young could identify.

Then folk music came to the churches. In 1964, Ray Repp, a Roman Catholic, wrote "Mass for Young Americans," which was quickly adopted and used by many progressive Catholic churches. It was the beginning of the folk mass, and there were many more to come.

Billy Graham, in 1965, introduced a movie entitled "The Restless Ones." The soundtrack was written by Ralph Carmichael, an early pioneer in contemporary gospel music. The music was soft by today's standards, but at the time of its release, the score was considered such hard rock that only Graham's name made it acceptable to the hard-core conservatives in the fundamentalist churches. The movie was a great success and was followed by "For Pete's Sake," from which came the song, "All My Life." This song was not only accepted by the churches, but subsequently was used by those same churches' choirs in their services.

"Good News" was an hour-long folk musical, written by Bob Oldenburg and others and performed in 1967 at a Southern Baptist retreat in Glorietta, New Mexico, under the direction of Billy Ray Hearn. This folk musical was so successful that Hearn took his youthful choir and toured 20 European cities, including a performance before 6,000 international Baptists at the World Baptist Youth Conference at Berne, Switzerland. This particular folk musical made a great impact in that it was accepted by the youth of America and Europe, and it satisfied the requirements of the older Baptists by ending with an altar call, the conclusion to any decent Baptist service.

"Life" was another well-received folk musical and was written by Otis Skillings. Ralph Carmichael, in 1969, chose to venture into the folk musical field, and with Word recording artist Kurt Kaiser wrote "Tell It Like It Is." It proved to be a big hit and sold hundreds of thousands of copies. The team wrote other musicals together and produced "Natural High," which was not within the confines of "folk" music. 1971 found Jimmy Owens' "Show Me" a California success with the youth. He and his wife, Carol, collaborated on "Come Together," one of the most utilized musicals of its type. Youth groups across the nation performed this work with great effect and achievement.

As in the early days when Aldine Kieffer printed *The Musical Million* to send out the news of what was happening in shape note music, in 1971 a Jesus music newspaper began its career to promote its interpretation of gospel. *Rock-n-Jesus* was published in Wichita, Kansas. *Harmony* and *Gospel Trade* have joined *Rock-n-Jesus* as contemporary gospel tradepapers, with more than 20 different types now on the market. Country music, not to be excluded, produces *Nashville Gospel*, which features the country artists who are deep into the gospel scene. In the same year a Jesus music oriented recording company saw its birth in California. It was the next logical step in a new and growing form of music, and its birthplace was most apt, since Jesus music originated primarily from that state.

Near the Costa Mesa area, a church had been built with the common name, Calvary Chapel. Its name was the only thing common about it. It was a church directed toward young people, and hordes of them began attending in blue jeans and casual dress. Today thousands of people, mostly young, attend the services at Calvary Chapel each Sunday. There were many musicians in the church, and Love Song, the first successful Jesus group, was nearby, so it was inevitable that Marantha Music Company should be formed.

In 1971, "The Everlasting Living Jesus Music Concert," their first album, was released. It was unique in that the music was performed not just by musicians who liked rock, but by those who professed to believe in Christ—an all-Christian effort. It was a smash hit and came to be known to those in the Jesus music circles simply as Marantha I. Love Song was among the groups appearing on the album.

This new form of religious music was not unknown to the gospel music industry. Word, Inc., in Waco, Texas, established a new label expressly for Jesus music. Marvin Norcross, president of Canaan Records, a branch of Word, Inc., was president of the GMA in 1974 and serves yet on its board. Word, with its auxiliary branches, is the world's biggest recording company, and Jesus music was in with the best in gospel music. The new Jesus label, Myrrh, started with Randy Matthews, son of Monty Matthews of the original Jordanaires, who was already well known in his field, and today has a vast number of young performers, among them a young girl with the unlikely name of Honeytree, who always manages to have a hit on the charts.

Another prominent artist in this field, Larry Norman, was from San Jose and began his writing career in 1969. He started out with a young recording company in California, Creative Sound, which is known today as Sonrise Mercantile. As could be predicted, Nashville was not to be left out of the new sound, and bought his album "Upon This Rock." Now writer and singer, Norman was called "the top solo artist in his field" by *Time* magazine. *Billboard* said, "Larry Norman is probably the most important songwriter since Paul Simon." This man grew with the grass roots of Jesus music and was one of its earliest pioneers. He began an extensive feat when he wrote the first contemporary Jesus opera. The opera was done in three parts. The first album, "So Long Ago the Garden," dealt with the past. "Only Visiting the Planet" was the second and addressed itself to the present. The trilogy was completed with "Another Land," which presents Norman's impressions of the future.

Each album in the triology ends with the title song and points to the next record's theme. Norman refers to the three-record set as a "total concept" work. "Another Land" deals with the Second Coming and the end times. Many different styles of music are incorporated into the music, reminiscent of "Jesus Christ: Superstar." The victorious theme is expressed in vaudevillian, early rock of the fifties, hard rock with an emphasis on electronics, and simple tunes with a well-defined melody. There is a great deal of symbolism in the work, which is a popular method employed by several of the Jesus music writers, including Andrew Culverwell.

Earlier much was said of Homer Rodeheaver, singing teacher, evangelist, and writer. His base for his gospel endeavors was at Winona Lake, Indiana. In 1976, years after the time of Mr. Rodeheaver, a film was produced at that same location which proved to be very important to contemporary music. Ken Anderson produced "Say It With Music," a film which boasted many artists and included comments and testimonies by a number of those same artists. Among those included were: The Imperials, Honeytree, Johnny Mann, The Archers, Steve Camp, John Hall, The Continentals, and Randy Matthews. The narrator of this production was none other than Ralph Carmichael. Several firsts by Carmichael have already been mentioned. He took traditional to contemporary, and one of his best vehicles was the song "He's Everything to Me" from Graham's movie "The Restless Ones." All those connected with this film had one purpose in mind, to get their message across. They used traditional and contemporary music, soft and hard rock, to convey their common belief.

A return to the very first method of producing gospel music is found in a statement made by Randy Matthews and published in *Harmony* magazine,

July/August, 1976: "What I'm saying is not new; the message has been given over and over again in different ways since the time of Jesus. In fact, Isaac Watts, one of the great hymn writers, did it when he said, 'My people have no music to sing. They're singing lewd, filthy songs of the street. All I'm doing is taking the music of my people and putting the message of Jesus to it.' And I say, 'Right on, Isaac,' that's all I'm doing. And it's not that radical the way I'm doing it."

There are a number of rock stations playing Jesus music. Many FM stations play blocks on Sunday morning, while others intersperse Jesus records among the secular songs. Approximately 92 radio stations in the United States and one in Puerto Rico have a complete gospel format, and there are thousands of other stations which play the brand of gospel most popular in their area, using one of the varying methods. Some have a "hymn" of the hour that may range from George Beverly Shay to contemporary or traditional gospel.

The Christian Broadcasting Network, located in Virginia Beach, Virginia, is soon to become the fourth major television network. Most prominent gospel singers have appeared on "The 700 Club," hosted by Pat Robertson and broadcast daily on CBN. CBN Center, now under construction in Virginia Beach, will house the network's headquarters, television studios, and production facilities, as well as the international satellite center and the international conference center; CBN University will offer graduate studies in theology and communications.

However, outside the Bible Belt, gospel radio has changed. In past years, gospel meant only the Southern traditional type of music, but today most stations play a middle-of-the-road selection. The artists will vary from Gaither to Marijohn Wilkins.

From its inception, gospel music was usually accompanied only by a piano, with perhaps a guitar or banjo or organ. Now it has become as sophisticated as secular music in its instrumentation and arrangement. The sound is more professional, and attracts those from 14 to 40, some of whom had not been gospel fans before. Today's parent generation grew up with Elvis Presley and the birth of rock and roll music. Their children have chosen a harder sound, a louder beat, but it is rock all the same. So those who were once negative toward quartet singing, particularly those who were not Southerners, now enjoy the music of such artists as Evie Tornquist, The Good News Circle, Jerry Arhelger, and the Jeremiah People, among others. The contemporary treatment of much of today's gospel music has won around those who were not nurtured in the old shape note singing tradition.

There is one thing that gospel music lacks, and will in all probability correct in the near future. It is the only popular form of music which does not have an accurate top 40 list from which the disc jockeys can pick and choose. Each of the all-gospel format stations makes up its own list of hits or else accepts the ones found in the trade papers, all of which vary greatly. The traditional and the contemporary papers go with the artists who fit their particular tastes. Consequently, the top 40 charts in each trade publication are almost completely different. A few names may appear in each, but there is no standard listing to be found.

The GMA is aware of the problems which radio stations are having in their efforts to please their individual audiences. The fifth annual Gospel Radio Seminar was held May 6 and 7, 1977, in Nashville. The theme for this seminar was "Realizing Your Potential." The speakers are always representatives of the various record companies (as well as members of the GMA) and the cost is held at a minimum so that even the smallest station can afford to take advantage of the opportunity. The recent cost was 30 dollars for broadcasters and 50 dollars for music industry personnel. It is hoped that by getting together with the radio personnel from all over the country and offering workshops on varying aspects of broadcasting, the GMA can help with new format ideas and general tips for better programming.

From encouragement by the GMA, gospel music has spread from concert hall and media airing to new and diverse areas. Christian supper clubs are slowly opening up across the country. With dinner comes the entertainment of gospel artists. Songs of Joy Club opened in Nashville in July of 1977. Among the people who have performed there are: Willie Wynn (formerly of the Oaks) and the Tennesseans, Betty Jean Robinson, Jerry and the Singing Goffs, the Lewis Family (bluegrass singers), the Hemphills (traditional), and Our Brothers Keeper (contemporary).

Delta and American Airlines now include a program of gospel music on their flights.

November 1977 was proclaimed Gospel Music Month by the governors of the following states: Alabama, California, Georgia, Louisiana, Mississippi, Nevada, New Mexico, North Carolina, Oklahoma, Vermont, and Virginia. The GMA is talking to governors in other states with the hope that they, too, will join in making this an annual tradition.

An institution has been mentioned many times in this work, although it has never been clearly defined; the reason being that it has never existed physically, but only in the hearts of those who have fought for its existence. The Gospel Music Hall of Fame for many years has been merely the dream of the GMA and all lovers of gospel music.

In 1967, a charter was drawn up by a few leaders in the GMA who believed that their dream of a structure housing the artifacts of gospel music could become a reality. Members, deceased and living, were first inducted into the Hall as early as 1971, even though there was no existing building in which to put likenesses and memorabilia of these individuals. Yet, the practice of recognizing the giants of the industry had begun.

A board of trustees, 11 people well-versed and oriented in gospel music, was appointed in August 1975 by the GMA, with four advisors in assistance. This board was organized to raise funds and work toward the realization of a hope long nursed and never forgotten. The trustees named Meurice LeFevre (son of Urias and Eva Mae) chairman; J. D. Sumner, vice-chairman; John Rees, treasurer; and Don Butler, chairman of fund raising. The following October at the National Quartet Convention, the public was made aware of these plans, and over 8,000 dollars were pledged. Some of this amount has been met, and monthly payments are still coming in. The fans at the convention were also informed of a different type of donation. For five dollars, they would receive a certificate for one square foot of the construction site. The Honorary Warranty

Deeds were numbered, signed by a representative of the Gospel Music Hall of Fame, and were offered as mementos of each person's contribution to the dream.

The construction site is directly across from the Country Music Hall of Fame at the point of entry into "Music Row" in Nashville. Negotiations were completed with an architect and a contractor in Nashville. On Saturday, October 9, 1976, the ground-breaking ceremonies were held, and construction has begun with the hope that the building would be completed in the spring of 1978.

In addition to the fans still securing deeds, big businesses have made contributions to the funding of this institution. BMI gave 10,000 dollars, a tax write-off to an industry which nets them thousands of dollars a year, a conservative estimate. The Don Light Talent Agency, the first all-gospel booking agency, also contributed 10,000 dollars. These presentations were made to Don Butler, Executive Director of the GMA and the Hall of Fame.

Telethons have long since been vehicles for soliciting money for worthy causes, and those connected with the funding of the Hall did not neglect its possibilities. January 15 and 16 of 1977 were the dates, and the Four-Star Building on Music Row via Opryland's Mobile Unit gave WZTV, Channel 17, Nashville, the location of the telethon.

It was considered a success. About 54,000 dollars in gifts and monthly pledges were accumulated. During the 40 hours of broadcast time, artists from several areas of gospel music performed. The Blackwood Brothers, the Downings, Willie Wynn and the Tennesseans brought a familiar flavor, as Randy Matthews and Dogwood gave a contemporary touch. Black gospel was represented by The Johnson Ensemble, The New World Singers, and several other groups. Country music came through with such notables as Roy Acuff, Skeeter Davis, Minnie Pearl, Connie Smith, Jeannie C. Riley, and many more. Music industry executives abounded, with officials from ASCAP, SESAC, Canaanland Music, Benson Publishing, "Record World," and other agencies and companies. Two men already inducted into the Hall of Fame were present, James Blackwood and Lee Roy Abernathy. However, the amount collected to date is insufficient, and the GMA is urging all its members to purchase more Warranty Deeds.

When finished, the Hall will consist of several departments. There will, of course, be a museum, which will include busts of the inducted members, manuscripts, diaries, pictures, instruments, and general memorabilia of the pioneers and the greats in the industry. Also there will be a wall plaque listing the names of all patrons and founder sponsors in addition to the charter members of the Hall.

Included will be a library, which will contain all phases of gospel music in songbook, informational material, and reference and research works for the benefit of church music directors, professionals, or for other interested people.

In one area a chapel will be erected, which will have twice-weekly services of an interdenominational theme, and will be open each day for personal prayer and meditation.

A theater complete with multi-media equipment will give to all visitors access to the various sounds and styles of gospel and sacred music.

The Nashville building will become the international headquarters for the GMA, and from this office the operation and planning of the radio seminars, workshops, general business, and promotional efforts will be based.

Inductions into the Hall of Fame come as a result of a structured system. They are first nominated by a 12-member committee whose qualifications for their position consist of 10 years active service in the field and who must be recognized for their accomplishments and be knowledgeable in one or more aspects of gospel music. The electors always come from different fields within the business, and live in diverse geographical locations. A panel of 100 Hall of Fame Electors is chosen by the GMA Board to vote on the winners.

Many of the names which have appeared in this volume are already members of the Hall, and those who have given their lifework to gospel music will, if not already included, become its members so that the followers of gospel will never forget their contributions and efforts across the years.

★ ★ ★

Gospel music is an open vessel, receptive to the innovations of the age. Through the years the sounds and methods of projecting this music have changed and altered with the times. The only thing that has remained unchanged is its message and its purpose.

Beginning in the middle 1960s and continuing to the present day, gospel music has again been shifting with the prevailing currents. The younger generation was aware of this movement from the onset, but many of the parent and grandparent set were not fully conscious of the new transformations until the Dove Awards Presentations in October, 1976.

At that time, the awards were given for the best performances and results in the bicentennial year. Since the provenance of the Dove in 1969, there had always been one award given for the best record album of the year. Not long before presentation time in 1976, it was announced that this tradition would be broken by dividing the category into four sections: Southern traditional, contemporary, inspirational, and performance by a non-gospel artist.

This decision came as quite a shock to many who had no inclination that henceforth gospel would become a generic term inclusive of many different types of music. Gospel had always been gospel. Now, suddenly, it had become categorized, an innovation never before conceived.

The winners, as conferred at the annual banquet on October 4, 1976, are as follows:

Best Gospel Record Album of the Year, Contemporary:
"No Shortage"...The Imperials
Best Gospel Record Album of the Year, Southern Traditional:
"Between the Cross and Heaven"...The Speer Family
Best Gospel Record Album of the Year, Inspirational:
"Jesus, We Just Want to Thank You"...The Bill Gaither Trio
Best Gospel Record Album of the Year, Non-Gospel Artist:
"Sunday Morning"...Charley Pride

This was the first time in the history of the Dove elections that the GMA membership at large was not allowed to vote. In previous years, membership into the GMA had automatically brought with it a ballot for the awards. But, as has been previously mentioned, it was decided by the GMA Board that only those within the industry would be allowed to cast a vote. The outcome of this first election which excluded the fans brought some notable changes in the results.

James Blackwood's record of six straight wins for Best Male Vocalist was upset by Johnny Cook, a tenor who sang for the Happy Goodmans, went solo, and is now back with the Goodman Family. Bill Gaither continued his seven-year tenure as Best Gospel Songwriter of the Year, while Neil Enloe's "Statue of Liberty" also took Best Gospel Song of the Year.

The Speer Family, after five consecutive wins and a loss to the Gaither Trio, took back Best Mixed Group. The Imperials came away with Best Male Gospel Group, Joy McGuire (who was with the Downings at the time) took Best Female Vocalist, and Henry Slaughter received Best Gospel Instrumentalist, giving him four victories in that field. There are 16 categories in all. The others deal with disc jockeys, TV programs, backliner notes, graphic layout and design, and cover photo, or cover art on a gospel album.

The new classification for non-gospel artist was made inevitable by the market flooding of many singers from the country and western field, Broadway, and TV. Among those to jump on the gospel wagon from the country field are: Tennessee Ernie Ford, Ray Price, Loretta Lynn, Hank Snow, Grandpa Jones, Betty Jean Robinson, Wanda Jackson, and Marilyn Sellers. Marijohn Wilkins and Kris Kristofferson teamed up on the hit "One Day At a Time," although each has had single hits. Pat Boone, who has been doing concerts with his family, has placed a firm emphasis on gospel music. Carol Lawrence of Broadway fame, and Norma Zimmer, the champagne lady, along with controversial Anita Bryant entered the gospel field with albums reflective of their respective talents, and after appearing with Billy Graham in various crusades. Both Norma Zimmer and Anita Bryant have new books out which comment on their personal beliefs and motives.

The results of the 1977 Dove Awards are as follows:

Best Gospel Record Album of the Year, Contemporary:
"Reba—Flash—Lady"...Reba Rambo Gardner
Best Gospel Record Album of the Year: Southern Traditional:
"Then and Now"...Cathedral Quartet
Best Gospel Album of the Year, Inspirational:
"Ovation"...Couriers
Best Gospel Record Album of the Year, Non-Gospel Artist:
"Home, Where I Belong"...B. J. Thomas
Best Gospel Record Album of the Year, Soul:
"This is Another Day"...Andrae Crouch
Best Male Gospel Group:
Cathedral Quartet
Best Mixed Gospel Group:
Speer Family

Best Male Vocalist:
James Blackwood
Best Female Vocalist:
Evie Tornquist
Best Gospel Song of the Year:
"Learning to Lean" by John Stallings
Gospel Songwriter of the Year:
Bill Gaither
Best Gospel Instrumentalist:
Henry Slaughter

For the record, the Speers have seven Doves as does James Blackwood. Bill Gaither has eight while his concert partner, Henry Slaughter, has five. However, there were several new names on the winners' roster, the Cathedral Quartet, Reba Rambo Gardner, Evie Tornquist, the Couriers, and Andrae Crouch.

The training which Glen Payne, manager of the Cathedral Quartet, received from Frank Stamps so many years ago has materialized into recognition from his peers. Consequently, as modernized as gospel music may be, its roots still remain in the early teaching and leadership of its pioneers.

The fan today who shops the gospel record section at most any store will find names which never before visited that area. The four currently defined areas of gospel music are often overlapped by many artists. The top 40 lists for each division will repeat quite a few names, so that with the exception of a diminishing number of gospel singers, artists may appear in two or three sections. And now there is one more to come.

Black has always been black and white has always been white as far as gospel music was concerned. A few individuals managed to cross over the color lines as performers, but otherwise, the two types of music have been separate entities.

In March of 1977 the invisible line was crossed when Bud Howell, Rick McGruder, and Shannon Williams of Nashboro Records became the first black gospel industry executives to join the GMA. Radio and TV have been combining the two styles of music over the past few years, and the hope now is that the offering of both types will increase concert audiences and album sales. Black gospel music has never been as organized or as widely promoted as has white, and the black performers who have never had the opportunity before to sing before mixed audiences will gain a new experience, as will the audiences themselves. Many gospel music fans are unaware of and unfamiliar with the artists of black gospel. The merger will provide something new and different for singer and listener alike.

Howell, McGruder, and Williams made a contribution to the Gospel Music Hall of Fame, and that institution has promised to give exposure to black artists and writers who have earned credit for their work over the past years. The alliance of the two types of music has necessitated an additional category in the Dove Awards for Record Album of the Year. In addition to the existing four divisions, there will be a soul division, bringing the categories in the Dove award to five. In another departure from past tradition, the 1977 Dove Awards

Banquet was not held in conjunction with the annual National Quartet Convention which falls the first week of every October. In 1977, the banquet occurred on November 29 at the Hyatt-Regency Hotel, Nashville.

* * *

Although this work has dealt solely with gospel music, it would be unthinkable not to mention the passing of Elvis Presley in August 1977. It has long been known that Presley was a devout gospel fan. In his early years, he chose the Jordanaires, a gospel quartet, to back him on his recordings. Through the two decades of his success, he remained a loyal fan, and often went to gospel concerts in disguise, many times slipping through the back door to avoid disclosing his presence.

In 1972 he began a business relationship with J. D. Sumner, the "granddaddy" of bass singers. Elvis Presley had been a follower of J. D. Sumner for many years, and at that time arranged for J. D. and the Stamps Quartet to back him on all future recordings and personal appearances. J. D.'s deep bass voice came across loud and clear on Elvis' records, and a warm personal friendship developed between the two.

In one television special on Elvis, there was a segment in which the legendary star was relaxing with J. D. and the other singers around a piano, harmonizing on some of the old gospel favorites. Elvis cut several gospel and hymn records, and in one of the last televised concerts before his death, people were picked at random to comment about why they were Elvis fans. Many of those who spoke remarked that they felt that there was a very real sincerity behind his singing of the gospel tunes. The general feeling seemed to be that the superstar believed in what he sang, and impressed that emotion upon those who listened.

Gospel music, as well as the rest of the world, is diminished by the passing of this great entertainer. However, some men are missed more than others, and the joy and happiness Elvis Presley gave to millions is his eulogy in itself. His contribution to American music surpasses words, only feeling is left, and each person whom Elvis touched will remember that feeling.

* * *

From the Puritan dissenters, to the camp meeting revivalists, to the intrepid teachers and singers who took gospel music over the next mountain and across the next flatland, we have come to sophisticated production numbers, space-age buildings housing an enormous industry, and a globe criss-crossed by gospel musicians. However, with the change, the complexity, and the prevalent modes, one thing remains the same, the people; not all of them to be sure, but enough so that the personal touch has not been lost.

The unique characteristic of hand meeting hand, emotion meeting emotion, prevails yet in a true gospel singing. As genes propagate life into life, gospel music has procreated itself through its offspring and its adherents so that the song goes on. As long as friendship, consideration, and concern are present between performer and listener, then gospel music lives. Fads will come and go.

The year of "Star Wars" and Kiss will pass, but the timelessness and sincerity of the communion of lovers of gospel will not fade and extinguish. The faithful will abide, and the chaff will blow away with the winds of the unworthy. Gospel music has altered, and will fluctuate with the times, but the love it brings, and the love of those who receive it will never vanish.

James Blackwood sings for himself and for the people. Since not many have the strong lead voice, he sounds the notes, but he also invites all present to share with him in the joy of his song and in the happiness received in its singing. Most of us have difficulty in keeping the melody to "Whispering Hope," and certainly have no aspiration to ever sing professionally, so we are fortunate that there are those who can do it for us and can express in music what we feel. And since it is an expression of our own feelings, the singer and the listener have now become united with corresponding emotions and a sense of having shared something very special. The people in the auditorium that night in Greenville found his quartet in general and James Blackwood in particular, to be most receptive to their moods and attitudes.

This is gospel music: the people moving toward the man who has led them to this experience, and the man singing with hands outstretched to them in welcome.

Bibliography

Books

Bailey, Albert Edward. *The Gospel in Hymns*. New York: Charles
    Scribner & Sons, 1950.

Baxter, Mrs. J. P., and Videt Polk. *Gospel Song Writers Biography*. Dallas, Texas:
    Stamps-Baxter Music and Printing Company, 1971.

Blum, John M., and others. *The National Experience: Part One* and *The National
    Experience: Part Two*. New York: Harcourt, Brace, & World, Inc.,
    1963, 1968, Second Edition.

Boni, Margaret Bradford, ed. *Fireside Book of Folk Songs*. New York:
    Simon & Schuster, Inc., 1947.

Burt, Jesse, and Duane Allen. *The History of Gospel Music*. Nashville:
    K & S Press, 1971.

Bushman, Richard L., ed. *The Great Awakening*. New York: Atheneum, 1970.

Carawan, Guy, and Candie Carawan, eds. *Voices From the Mountains*. New
    York: Alfred A. Knopf, Inc., 1975.

Chase, Gilbert. *America's Music*. New York: McGraw-Hill Book Company,
    1955, 1966. Revised second edition.

Chitwood, Oliver Perry. *A History of Colonial America*. New York:
    Harper & Brothers, 1931, 1948. Second Edition.

Combs, Josiah H. *Folk-Songs of the Southern United States*. Austin:
    University of Texas Printing Division, 1967.

Cuney-Hare, Maud. *Negro Musicians and Their Music*. New York:
    Da Capo Press, 1974.

de Luma, Dominique-Rene. *Reflections on Afro-American Music*. Kent, Ohio:
    The Kent State University Press, 1973.

Eisenstadt, Abraham S. *American History: Recent Interpretations*. New York:
    Thomas A. Crowell Company, 1969. Second Edition.

Fenner, Thomas P. *Religious Folk Songs of the Negro.* Hampton, Virginia: The Hampton Normal and Agricultural Institute, 1909. Second Edition.

Gentry, Linnell. *A History and Encyclopedia of Country, Western, and Gospel Music.* St. Clair Shores, Michigan: Scholarly Press, Inc., 1972.

Haralaambos, Michael. *Right On: From Blues to Soul in Black America.* New York: Drake Publishers Inc., 1975.

Ives, Burl. *Song in America.* New York: Duell, Sloan, & Pearce, 1962.

Jackson, George Pullen. *Another Sheaf of White Spirituals.* Gainesville, Florida: University of Florida Press, 1952.

————. *Spiritual Folk-Songs of Early America.* New York: J. J. Augustin, 1937.

————. *White and Negro Spirituals.* New York: J. J. Augustin, 1943.

————. *White Spirituals in the Southern Uplands.* New York: Dover Publications, Inc., 1965.

Kennedy, R. Emmet. *More Mellows.* New York: Dodd-Mead & Company, 1931.

Lang, Paul Henry, ed. *One Hundred Years of Music In America.* New York: G. Scheriner, Inc., 1961.

Leish, Kenneth W., and Charles W. Felds, eds. *The American Heritage Songbook.* New York: American Heritage Publishing Company, Inc., 1969.

Locke, Alain. *The Negro and His Music—Negro Art: Past and Present.* New York: Arno Press and The New York Times, 1969.

Lomax, Alan, and John A. Lomax. *Folk Song: USA.* New York: Grosset & Dunlap, 1947.

————. *The Folk Songs of North America.* Garden City, New York: Doubleday & Company, Inc., 1960.

————. *Hard Hitting Songs for Hard-Hit People.* New York: Oak Publications, 1967.

Luboff, Norman, and W. Stracke. *Songs of Man.* New York: Walton Music Corporation, 1969.

Marrocco, W. Thomas, and Harold Gleason, eds. *Music in America.* New York: W. W. Norton & Company, 1964.

Mattfeld, Julius. *Variety Music Cavalcade.* Englewood Cliffs, New Jersey: Prentice Hall, Inc., 1971. Third Edition.

Miller, John C., ed. *The Colonial Image.* New York: George Braziller, Inc., 1962.

Morgan, Edmund S. *The Puritan Family.* New York: Harper & Row, Publishers, 1944, 1966.

McLuhan, Marshall. *Understanding Media.* New York: New American Library, Inc. 1964. Re-print of hardcover edition by McGraw-Hill Book Company.

Okum, Milton. *Something To Sing About!* New York: The MacMillan Company, 1968.

Pederson, Duane. *Jesus People.* Glendale, California: G/L Publications, 1971.

Racine, Kree Jack. *Above All.* Memphis: Jarodoce Publications, 1967.

Bibliography

Roszak, Theodore. *The Making of a Counter Culture.* New York: Doubleday & Company, 1969.

Rublowsky, John. *Music in America.* New York: The MacMillan Company, 1967.

Southern, Eileen, ed. *Readings in Black American Music.* New York: W. W. Norton & Company, Inc., 1971.

Wright, Louis B. *The Cultural Life of the American Colonies.* New York: Harper & Row, 1957.

Magazines

Baker, Paul, "California Dreaming," *Harmony,* July-August 1976, 22.

Mangano, Phil, "Record Reviews," *Harmony,* July-August 1976, 24.

Smith, Sam, "Say It With Music...Say It With Film," *Harmony,* July-August 1976, 14-15.

Newsletters

Good News, January 1977, April 1977, June 1977.

Index

Index

Index

Index

Index

Index

Index

Index

Index

Index

461